Landscapes of

LA PALMA
AND EL HIERRO

a countryside guide

Fifth edition

Noel Rochford

SUNFLOWER BOOKS

Fifth edition © 2009
Sunflower Books™
PO Box 36160
London SW7 3WS, UK
www.sunflowerbooks.co.uk

Windmill near Las Tricias (Walk 15)

ISBN 978-1-85691-365-2

Important note to the reader

We have tried to ensure that the descriptions and maps in this book are error-free at press date. The book will be updated, where necessary, whenever future printings permit. It will be very helpful for us to receive your comments (sent in care of the publishers, please) for the updating of future printings. *Note that all island roads were renumbered just before press date; our maps and text show the new numbers, but signposting on the ground may differ for some time!*

   We also rely on those who use this book — especially walkers — to take along a good supply of common sense when they explore. Conditions change fairly rapidly in the Canary Islands, and *storm damage or bulldozing may make a route unsafe at any time*. If the route is not as we outline it here, and your way ahead is not secure, return to the point of departure. *Never attempt to complete a tour or walk under hazardous conditions!* Please read carefully the notes on pages 36 to 41, as well as the introductory comments at the beginning of each tour and walk (regarding road conditions, equipment, grade, distances and time, etc). Explore *safely*, while at the same time respecting the beauty of the countryside.

Cover photograph: in La Palma's banana groves
Title page: sabina, *a native juniper*

Photographs: Noel Rochford (except page 18: Conny Spelbrink)
Maps: Sunflower Books, based on 1:50,000 Spanish military maps (with permission of the Servicio Geográfico del Ejército)
Drawings: Sharon Rochford
A CIP catalogue record for this book is available from the British Library.
Printed and bound in China: WKT Company Ltd.

✿ Contents

4   Landscapes of La Palma and El Hierro

Market in Santa Cruz

Preface

For most tourists in Britain, the Canary Islands mean Tenerife, Gran Canaria, Lanzarote and Fuerteventura. But there are actually seven islands in the archipelago. Lesser-known La Gomera, La Palma and El Hierro are still utopias for nature lovers. They are as yet unspoilt.

They lack the fine glistening beaches of the more popular islands, and this may be their saving grace. It's unlikely that mainstream tourism will ever reach them. Great news for those of us who seek peace and quiet.

In natural beauty, La Palma rivals all the other islands put together. Its immense, abyss-like crater, the Caldera de Taburiente (which geologists now refer to as an enormous landslide), is one of the largest of its kind in the world. Deep within its pine-speckled, towering walls is a year-round abundance of water — gushing streams, boisterous cascades, and a plummeting waterfall. Outside the crater, high on the cloud-catching hillsides, two million-year-old laurel forests grow as dense as jungle. In the southern half of the island, hills pitted with volcanic craters, and mini-deserts of black *lapilli* speak of the island's volcanic past. This stark, striking landscape, all the more dramatic for its stabs of volcanic reds, oranges, and yellows, is far removed from the lush and verdant, tree-clad north.

Landing on El Hierro by boat many years ago, I wondered what I had let myself in for. Before me stood a dried-up, sprawling mountain of rock, rising straight from the sea, treeless and barren. Tired stone walls stretched half-heartedly across steep sea slopes … the only hint of civilisation. But day by day the island's charms revealed themselves: dramatic cliff top views, highland pastures shrouded in mist, countryside littered with volcanic cones, a maze of stone walls, turquoise-green rock pools, delightful rustic villages, venerable Canary pines and wizened junipers. These were but a few of the island's unpublicised treasures. And where else would your taxi driver buy *you* lunch? Still little touched by tourism, El Hierro is by far the friendliest place in the Canaries.

If you want a holiday with razzmatazz, head for one of the 'big four' (with the appropriate *Landscapes* guide). But if you don't mind unrushed service, and if you want to return home more relaxed than when you left, then start packing. Discover La Gomera with *Landscapes of Southern Tenerife and La Gomera,* or use this book to enjoy the best of La Palma and El Hierro.

Acknowledgements

Special thanks to the following people for their invaluable help: Conny Spelbrink, who lives on La Palma and sends frequent updates; the Oficina de Turismo, El Hierro; Medio Ambiente, La Palma and El Hierro; my sister Sharon, for her illustrations of island flora.

Recommended reading

There are no general guides devoted specifically to these islands, but any general guide to the Canary Islands should prove useful for history and practicalities. Try to buy a copy of Bramwell's *Wild flowers of the Canary Islands* on the island, or look for it in your library.

Useful websites

www.lapalma.turismo.com (La Palma Tourist Board)
www.el-hierro.org (El Hierro Tourist Board)
www.iac.es (see photo caption on page 18)
www.ecoturismocanarias.com (country cottages to rent)
See also page 134 for flight and ferry websites.

Walk 10: Ascending Pico Bejenado, near the Mirador El Rodeo

● Picnicking

La Palma and El Hierro are rugged and unspoilt, ideal for picnicking. On the following pages I have listed a few of my favourite picnic spots along the routes of the walks. All the information you need to get there is given on the following pages, where *picnic numbers correspond to walk numbers*. Thus you can quickly find the general location on the islands by referring to the touring maps, where the walks are numbered in green. I give transport details (🚗: car parking; 🚌: how to get there by bus), walking times, and views or setting. Beside the picnic title, you will find a map reference: the location of the picnic spot is pinpointed on this *walking map* with the symbol *P*. All of the picnic places are illustrated.

Most of these picnic spots are reached after a very short, easy walk. In fact, they make *excellent rambles for 'non-walkers'*, and are ideal for stretching your legs during car tours. Do, however, look over the comments before setting out: if some walking is involved, remember to wear sensible shoes. Always take a **sunhat** with you (○ indicates a picnic in full sun). It's a good idea to take along a plastic sheet as well, in case the ground is damp or prickly.

All picnickers should read the Country code on page 38 and go quietly in the countryside.

La Palma

1 MIRADOR LA TOSCA (map page 44, photograph page 43)

by car: 15-25min on foot	by bus: 20-30min on foot

🚗 Park on the concrete lane about 0.5km east of the Mirador La Tosca (Car tour 1).
🚌 bus to the Mirador La Tosca (Línea 2).
Follow the beginning of Walk 1, down to a magnificent panorama over La Tosca and the distant sea-cliffs. Dragon trees galore; shade nearby.

3 LOS TILOS (map page 48, photographs pages 50, 51) 🛆

by car: 5-30min on foot	by bus: not easily accessible

🚗 Park at Los Tilos car park (Car tour 1).
Below the car park there is an organised picnic area — quiet except for weekends. But I prefer picnicking below it, alongside the watercourse (canal). To get there, refer to the notes in Walk 3, from the 1h45min-point. It's an excellent spot to explore. Then perhaps refer to Short walk 3-2 to explore the fascinating barranco *(which I find too busy with walking traffic for an enjoyable picnic).*

6 ERMITA DE LA VIRGEN DEL PINO (map page 63)

by car: 5-20min on foot   *by bus: not easily accessible*
🚗 Park in the car park at the chapel: take the LP302 for 'Parque Nacional'; the first right turn leads to the *ermita*. (Car tour 2)
Picnic in the forest of venerable Canary pines behind the chapel.

7a LA PARED VIEJA (map pages 68-69) 🛉

by car: up to 5min on foot   *by bus: not easily accessible*
🚗 Park at the picnic area. Turn left off the El Pilar/San Isidro road just under 5km northeast of the Refugio El Pilar (signposted). (Car tour 2)
An official picnic site in a dense laurel forest. Popular on weekends.

7b (REFUGIO) EL PILAR (map pages 68-69, photograph page 80) 🛉

by car: up to 5min on foot   *by bus: not easily accessible*
🚗 Park at the picnic area, off the El Pilar road (LP301), 7km south of the LP3 (Car tour 2).
An official picnic site in the woods at the foot of Pico Birigoyo.

7c LLANO DEL JABLE (map pages 68-69, photographs pages 67, 80)

by car: up to 5min on foot   *by bus: not easily accessible*
🚗 Park under the pines: turn right off the El Pilar road onto a gravel track just beyond Montaña Quemada, 4km south of the LP3 (a detour on Car tour 2).
Picnic under pines in this 'desert' of black lapilli. Avoid on windy days.

11 CALDERA DE TABURIENTE (map pages 88-89, photograph of the *barranco* opposite) ○

by car: 20-40min on foot
🚗 Park in the bed of the Barranco de las Angustias (Car tour 3).
Picnic anywhere along the barranco. *Some 20min upstream, you will find water in the river bed. There is some shade from the ravine walls about 40min upstream, by a small cascade and pool.*

Some organised picnic sites on La Palma

LAGUNA DE BARLOVENTO (map page 44; Car tour 1) △ ✖ 🛉

🚗 Park at the picnic site. Follow the LP109 southwest from Barlovento for 2km, then fork left to the picnic area.
Official site with full facilities, plus restaurant, camp ground and handicraft shop. A 'rural interpretation centre' is being built nearby.

FUENTE DE OLEN (touring map; Car tour 1) 🛉

🚗 Park at the site, off the LP4, 26km northwest of Santa Cruz
Set in pines, up high on the way to the cumbre; *full facilities.*

EL FAYAL (map page 106; Car tour 3) 🛉

🚗 Park at the site: turn left off the LP1 (signposted for Puntagorda) 1.5km north of the main Puntagorda turn-off (the turn-off to the picnic site is also the rear entrance to the village).
Located amidst pines and tree heather; full facilities.

MONTE BREÑA (touring map; Car tour 2) 🛉

🚗 Park at the site, off the LP202 south of San José.
An official site with full facilities.

MONTAÑA LAS TOSCAS (touring map; Car tour 2) 🛉

🚗 Park at the site; take the first right turn off the LP206 south of Mazo.
An official site (no toilets) on the slopes of Montaña Las Toscas.

El Hierro

18a MIRADOR DE JINAMA (map pages 116-117, photo page 118)

by car: 5-15min on foot   *by bus: 10-25min on foot*

🚗 Park at the *mirador* (Car tour 4).

🚌 towards Valverde from Tigaday; alight at the turn-off to the *mirador*. *Picnic on the hillside above the* mirador, *in the shade of pines. Or follow the path down towards Frontera for ten minutes, where you will find a belvedere with stone tables and benches (but no shade). There are stunning views here, but the return is steep.*

Below Dos Aguas in the Barranco de las Angustias (some two hours from the car park); the setting for Picnic 11 is similar.

18b ERMITA VIRGEN DE LA PEÑA (map pages 116-117, photographs below and page 120) ○

---

by car: 20-30min on foot   *by bus: 20-30min on foot*

🚗 Park at the Mirador de la Peña and walk up to the *ermita* (Car tour 4).

🚌 Guarazoca bus to the end of the route

Picnic overlooking El Golfo, alongside the chapel or along the path that descends to the sea, which is a minute above the chapel. One of the finest views in the archipelago, but very little shade.

19 MIRADOR DE LA LLANIA (map page 121, photo pages 122-123)

---

by car: 5-10min on foot   *by bus: 5-10min on foot*

🚗 Park off the HI1, by the road to the Ermita de la Virgen de los Reyes (Car tour 4).

🚌 towards Valverde from Tigaday; alight at the turn-off to the *ermita*.

Follow the sign for the mirador *and climb to the rim of the* cumbre, *for more stunning views over the crater. Use the notes for Walk 19 to see the exquisite wooded paths in the area. Plenty of shade nearby.*

20 MIRADOR DE LAS PLAYAS (map pages 128-129, photo page 126)

---

by car: up to 5min on foot   *by bus: 20-30min on foot*

🚗 Park at the the *mirador:* the turn-off lies south of San Andrés, 5km down the El Pinar/La Restinga road (Car tour 4).

🚌 La Restinga bus: alight at the turn-off to the *mirador*, 700m away.

Picnic near the mirador, *with its superb coastal view. Shade of pines.*

Some organised picnic sites on El Hierro

LAS PLAYAS (see touring map) 🍴

🚗 Park off the HI30 at Las Playas, 1.5km north of the *parador*.

An organised picnic site with a spectacular backdrop.

TIMIJIRAQUE (see touring map) 🍴

🚗 Park at the site, off the HI30 south of Puerto de la Estaca

An organised picnic site with facilities at one of the few sandy beaches on the island.

HOYA DEL MORCILLO (see touring map) 🍴

🚗 Park at the picnic area, 5.5km off the HI1 (Car tour 4)

An organised site with all facilities.

The Ermita Virgen de la Peña (Picnic 18b, Walk 18)

☀ *Touring*

The **public transport** network on La Palma is quite good and, by referring to the timetables on pages 131-133, you can plan some inexpensive touring itineraries. But on El Hierro, there are very few bus lines, despite recently increased services. Touring by **taxi** is another option, although a bit expensive. There are a few **coach tours** operating on La Palma, but none on El Hierro.

Hiring your own transport will be essential on El Hierro and the most convenient way to tour La Palma as well. Car hire is relatively inexpensive, but insurance is extra *and advisable.* Ask to see all the rental and insurance conditions (in English), and make sure you understand them. Carry the rental firm's telephone number (and a number where they can be reached outside office hours) with you. If you pay by credit card, remember to check the amount you sign for and keep all receipts!

The touring notes are brief: they include little history or other information that you can obtain in general guides or free from the local tourist offices. Instead, I've concentrated on the 'logistics' of touring: times and distances, road conditions, and seeing parts of the islands that many tourists miss. Most of all, I emphasise possibilities for **walking** and **picnicking** (the symbol *P* is used to alert you to a picnic spot; see pages 7-10). While some of the picnic and short walk suggestions may not be suitable during a long car tour, you may see a landscape that you would like to explore at leisure another day.

Most major **petrol stations** are open on Sundays and holidays, but a few of the smaller ones may not be. Take along **warm clothing** and some **food and drink**; be prepared for delays on the small country roads and tracks, and remember that mountain roads may sometimes be **impassable** in stormy weather. **Allow enough time**: the estimated driving times for each tour only includes brief stops at viewpoints labelled ☜.

The touring maps are designed to be held out facing the touring notes and contain all the information you need to follow the tours. But take time to look at the walking maps, too, when touring; they cover most of the islands in greater detail. The **symbols** in the text correspond to those on the touring maps: see map key.

1 LA PALMA'S VERDANT NORTH AND THE ISLAND'S SUMMITS

Santa Cruz • Los Sauces • Barlovento • Garafía • Roque de los Muchachos • Santa Cruz

190km/118mi; 7h driving; take the northern exit from Santa Cruz.

On route: ⊼ at Los Tilos, Laguna de Barlovento, Fuente de Olen; Picnics (see pages 7-10) 1, 3; Walks 1-6, 15, 16

The roads are generally very winding and, on a few stretches, narrow; some are country lanes, others might prove vertiginous for some motorists. This drive is not recommended immediately after heavy rainfall (especially in winter), due to the danger of rockfall. Where the road climbs above 600m, there's always the possibility of cloud. No petrol stations between Barlovento and Santa Cruz (133km on the touring route via the observatory). Be alert for ongoing roadworks in the north, also for livestock and pedestrians on all roads: drive slowly.

Opening hours

Los Tilos Interpretation Centre 09.00-17.00 daily (till 17.30 Jul-Oct); tel (922) 451246

Parque Cultural La Zarza 11.00-17.00 daily (till 19.00 July-Oct); tel (922) 695005

Observatorio Astrofísico open to the public on a few days in summer: for information telephone the observatory (922) 405500.

G aping, deep *barrancos* leave you in awe as you edge along the island's high sea shelf. The further north you go, the more desolate the landscape. Then, heading inland, you climb to the rim of the crater, up through

*Spring and shrine to
St John the Baptist
at Puntallana*

forest, to a moonscape of volcanic hues and unsurpassed panoramic views. It will be a long day, so take plenty of snacks … and plenty of film.

Heading north on the LP1 out of Santa Cruz, climb to the island's midriff (🅿 at 7.5km). At **Puntallana** (10km ⛪⊕) fork right into the village and, just before the church of St John the Baptist, descend a steep narrow lane to the right. Park 0.2km downhill, off the road, just before a T-junction. Traditional Canarian houses line the lane. Ivy and other creepers cascade down the ravine walls. Walk downhill a few minutes, then take the first right turn, to find a splendid little *plaza* shaded by a jacaranda tree, hidden in the *barranco* wall. A spring flows into small pools here, alongside a shrine to St John the Baptist.

Return to the LP1 and continue north, heading in and out of sheer-sided ravines and a series of tunnels. Less than 1km beyond **La Galga** (17km ✗), approaching a bend in the road, turn off right for the signposted **Mirador de San Bartolomé** (📷), passing the church of the same name (⛪) as you climb the hill. From this *mirador* there is a fine view inland, across the mountainous eastern wall that flanks the crater. Los Sauces is the settlement further north. Returning to the LP1, stop at the church of San

Bartolomé for a slightly unnerving cliff-edge view into the **Barranco de la Galga** (📷), then return to the main road and turn right. The track forking left just before the tunnel is the setting for Walk 5, an easy stroll up into the laurel woods. The oldest Guanche remains on La Palma, dating back to the 4th century BC, were discovered in the cave-like rock overhang you can see in the next big ravine, the **Barranco de San Juan**. The finds from this cave are exhibited in the museum at the San Francisco Convent in Santa Cruz.

At **Las Lomadas** (26.5km ✗) you reach a roundabout. Going straight ahead would take you to one of the most modern arched bridges in the world, a spectacular span 150m/500ft above the *barranco* bed (★). To the left is the turn-off for Los Nacientes (springs) de Marcos y Cordero — the first 4km on tarmac, then a rough track only suitable for four wheel drive vehicles. (Walk 4 ends here, emerging from the canyon that hides these mountain springs: if you're adventurous, fit and have a head for heights, make this walk a priority.) But for this tour, take the *next* left turn off the roundabout, for Los Tilos, and drive up another gaping *barranco,* the Barranco del Agua.

The hydroelectric plant up here is the only one in the archipelago. This immense dark ravine (see photograph page 47) boasts a magnificent jungle-thick laurel forest; there is also a colony of prehistoric *Woodwardia radicans* (ferns) on the gorge wall. You can learn more about La Palma's flora at the very basic visitor centre at **Los Tilos★** (30km *i*✗🍴; **P**3), and read more about this area on pages 45-51 (Walks 3 and 4).

Leaving the Barranco del Agua, continue north on the LP1 to La Palma's third largest town, **Los Sauces** (32km ♠♦✗🚐⊕), where Walk 2 begins and Walk 3 ends. This very pleasant (and principal) agricultural centre is swallowed up amidst banana groves. Some 1.5km out of town, branch off seaward for San Andrés (signposted). Descending through banana groves, you pass the signposted turn-off for Puerto Espíndola and Charco Azul, your route on the way back.

San Andrés (36km ♠♦✗) sits on the hillside just above the sea. The restaurant in the square serves good fresh fish. Wander along the cobbled lanes of the village, then peek inside the 17th-century church in the palm-graced *plaza*, to see some rather macabre wax models. These represent ailing or injured parts of the body. In a practice dating back to the Middle Ages, they are pinned to a board

Piscinas de la Fajana

on the church wall, in the hope that illnesses will be cured and injuries mended.

Return to the Puerto Espíndola junction and turn right; 0.5km further on, fork right again for the Charco Azul. Some 0.3km down this narrow lane, come to a parking bay overlooking this emerald-green natural rock-pool *(charco)*, set at the foot of low sea cliffs. *(Remember, however: when the seas are high, it's too dangerous even to venture down onto the rock here.)* Continuing on through banana groves, reach a junction and turn right into the new port of **Puerto Espíndola** (39.5km ✗), with an excellent restaurant, 'Meson del Mar'.

Ascending to the LP1, keep right all the way. Just over 2km north along the LP1 turn right for 'Faro de Punta Cumplida'. This narrow, winding and bumpy road will take you down to some more rock pools. Keep right at the T-junction; 1.2km down, at **Punta Talavera**, there's an inconspicuous little port concealed in a rocky promontory. Park above it and walk down to the fishermen's huts that snuggle below, and to the tunnel in the rock — a very scenic spot. Swimming is only safe here when the sea is calm. After passing the **Faro de Punta Cumplida**, you climb through extensive banana plantations to a T-junction, where you turn right and descend (🚐) to the **Piscinas de la Fajana** (50km ⬧✗△). The pools here, larger than those at the Charco Azul, are also set in the seashore lava and are equally dangerous when the sea is high. Walking beyond the apartments for 10 minutes, you will find some unfrequented natural pools set in a flat tongue of rough lava.

To rejoin the LP1, pass the turn-off left back to the lighthouse and keep straight uphill, ignoring all turn-offs. Turn right on the LP1 and climb to **Barlovento** (57.5km ✚✗🚌⊕), an exposed, windswept village with a thoroughfare the width of a motorway. Walk 2 ends here. Pass the LP1 off right to Gallegos and continue straight ahead for 1km, *past* the Hotel La Palma Romantica (58.5km ▲▲). When you come to La Pradera (59.5km ✗), a large prettified shed standing amidst trees off to the right, you may wish to 'go native': this cosy local restaurant is a brilliant lunch or snack stop. Try the excellent grilled cheese with *mojo* sauce and a glass of red wine. Just past the restaurant, take the turn-off left to the **Laguna de Barlovento** *zona recreativa* (☐✗), laid out at the side of the island's largest reservoir, with restaurant, shop selling handicrafts and local produce and a duck pond. A 'rural interpretation centre' is being built nearby. All sorts of birds gather in this area around the reservoir, and in the winter one can see many migrating birds as well.

Turn back from the picnic grounds and retrace your route for 3km, then fork left on the LP1 for Gallegos/ Franceses. After 0.5km you pass the turn-off to the Mirador de la Montaña del Molino, a viewpoint on the reddish hillock off to the right. Less than 1km further on is the **Mirador La Tosca** (65.5km ⬚*P*1), from where you have a superb view over La Tosca's dragon trees and along the wild north coast. Settlements are few and far between. Grazing is the main means of livelihood in this far-flung corner of the island. Walk 1, which starts from here, gives you a taste of this pastoral corner of the north.

Possible detours: The main tour passes above two

precious little villages, Gallegos and Franceses. But I highly recommend taking detours to them if you have the time: 2km for Gallegos and just over 5km for Franceses. Note that some of the roads are narrow and, in Franceses, some stretches of road are *vertiginous*. To make for Gallegos, where Walk 1 ends, turn right at 72.5km. Keep right on entering the village, turn sharp left at the village bar/shop (the first left turn you come to), and then remain on this road, climbing back up to the LP1. The flimsy sign announcing the Franceses turn-off (76km) comes up without warning. *This detour is recommended for confident drivers only.* It's a spectacular and rugged corner of the island, and relatively unvisited … so far! You'll pass various tiny *barrios* (parts of the village), each of them named. First you squeeze through Los Machines. Then, winding in and out of gullies, ignore a turn-off to La Fajana (although it is only 2.5km off the LP1, this very narrow road down to the coast is pretty hair-raising!). Less than

The Roque de los Muchachos, at 2426m/7960ft, is La Palma's highest peak. One of the paths from the car park leads to a nose of rock that juts out into the crater. Magnificent sweeping views await you, over the crater walls, the island's summits, and to El Hierro, La Gomera and Tenerife. Try to enjoy a sunset up here.

The Observatorio Astrofísico, near the Roque de los Muchachos, is the most important in the northern hemisphere. For fascinating details and information about visiting (in English), log on to www.iac.es.

1km further on, you round a bend at the edge of the enormous Barranco Traviesa and come upon a magnificent vista aross the coastal hills of the northwest. Then a steep climb takes you back up to the LP1, where you turn right.

The road snakes up through tree heather to 1100m/ 3600ft. Keep straight on, where the LP109 joins from the left. If you're ready for lunch, try the Bar/Restaurant Los Reyes in the tiny hamlet of **Roque del Faro**, 1.5km along. On cold days try the warming rabbit or goat stews, the broth, or the very tasty *gofio* dish (made from roasted maize). Wash it down with the wine called 'tea'. A great place, and as yet few tourists know about it.

Within the next 5km you reach the **Parque Cultural La Zarza★** (91km). The small well-equipped museum here (with explanations in English) is well worth a stop. A way-marked path (allow 15-20 minutes each way) heads off behind the museum to two 'caves' (La Zarza and La Zarcita, really rock overhangs), with curious Guanche petroglyphs★. The meaning of these spiralled rock carvings has still not been discovered, but it is thought that they have to do with water.

Continuing west, when you reach the Puntagorda/ Garafía junction (⊕ Cruz Roja), turn right. Notice the old *gofio* mill on the right here. A convoluted road (LP112) down through almond groves brings you to **Garafía** (101.5km ♣✕⊕), another isolated farming outpost, best known for breeding livestock. Reaching the village, turn right for the 16th-century church of Nuestra Señora de la Luz★, one of the largest on the island. It has an interesting wooden ceiling. Walk 16 begins and ends here ... but the truth is that few hikers venture out this far into the 'sticks'. Diners, there are two good restaurants here, both offering good, plain cooking in simple surroundings: Santo Domingo in the *plaza* and the restaurant El Bernegal, just outside the village on the road to Las Tricias.

Leaving Garafía, you can make a pleasant circuit by continuing past the square and taking the first right. Then turn right again, to return to the main road. Making for Las Tricias, turn right and follow the road south. Another *gofio* (maize) mill appears on the right as you leave Garafía. Once again settlement is sparse. Two more impressive ravines are crossed. Climbing slopes clad with almond trees, you pass through picturesque **Las Tricias★** (113km), a retreat for 'alternative life-stylers'. Walk 15 would take you right down amongst them all. But it's really the great clumps of dragon trees everyone comes to see (photograph page 104).

Just 1km above Las Tricias you meet the LP1 sign-posted back to Garafía. Turn left uphill here, to begin your ascent to the Roque de los Muchachos. After 10km branch off right on the LP4. The ascent gets steeper, the bends sharper. Stunning scenery unravels — over the farmlands of the north, the thickly wooded hillsides, and the sea. Nearer the rim of the crater, the pines vanish and *codeso* carpets the ground. Following signs for the observatory, turn right at the first junction and head up to the island's highest peak, the **Roque de los Muchachos★** (146km 📷). For a spectacular view into the Caldera de Taburiente, walk down to the salient of rock on the right, below the car park. Over the shoulder of the crater the white-domed buildings of the **Observatorio Astrofísico** glare back at you. This complex, the most important in the northern hemisphere, has 13 telescopes — two for the sun and the other ten for the furthest galaxies. The new Gran Telescopio Canarias (2007) is one of the largest telescopes in the world.

Return to the junction with the LP4 and turn right for Santa Cruz. Rounding the *caldera*, the deep volcanic yellows, oranges and reds in the rock distract you from the panoramic views. Two more *miradors* (**Los Andenes** and **Degollada de Franceses**) on the very edge of the crater (📷) give you another chance to take in this great work of nature. Descending, re-enter the pine zone and after 8km pass the Pico de la Nieve track, starting point for Walk 6 and Short walk 6. The Fuente de Olen picnic area (🛏) lies below the road less than 3km further on. Over the pines the east coast begins to open up and, lower down, you get a fine view of Santa Cruz, with a prominent half-crater backdrop. On reaching the LP401, keep left, then turn right on the LP1 into **Santa Cruz** (190km).

2 VOLCANIC SPLENDOURS IN THE SOUTH OF LA PALMA

Santa Cruz • Los Canarios (Fuencaliente) • El Paso • El Pilar • Santuario de las Nieves • Santa Cruz

134km/84mi; 5h driving; take the southern exit from Santa Cruz

On route: ⌷ at Las Toscas (Mazo), on the main road above Las Indias, Refugio El Pilar, La Pared Vieja; Picnics (see pages 7-10) 6, 7a-b, (7c); Walks 6-9, (10)

Driving will be slow, due to narrow winding roads. Watch out for pedestrians and livestock on the roads. The southern tip of the island can be very windy.

Opening hours
Mazo, market days: 15.00-19.00 Sat; 09.00-13.00 Sun
El Molino (ceramics centre): 09.00-17.00 Mon-Fri, except during lunch hours (13.00-15.00)
Cueva de Belmaco (archaeological museum) 10.00-18.00 (Mon-Sat), 10.00-15.00 (Sun)
Bodegas Teneguía: 08.00-14.00 and 15.00-17.00 Mon-Fri
National Park Visitor Centre: 09.00-14.00 and 16.00-18.30 daily, including holidays
Chipi Chipi Restaurant: 12.00-15.30 and 19.00-23.00 Tue-Sun; closed Mon and from 1/10 to 15/11.

You'll marvel at the volcanic landscapes on this tour, the kaleidoscope of scenery, and the striking colour contrasts. Gastronomic delights, plain but hearty, lie on route as well — indulge yourself.

Head south on the LP2, passing the long man-made Playa de Bajamar. The turn-off right to the Playa de los Cancajos (▲▲▲✗) lies 3km along: with its rock-studded coves, it is the best beach in the vicinity. Just 0.1km further on, turn right (Exit 2b) and, at a roundabout follow sign-posting for Los Canarios. Beyond the airport turn-off, you head through colourful **San Antonio** (4.5km ▲✗). Some 1.5km further on, you come to a junction. The main tour continues to the right here, up into the hills (LP206, sign-posted to San José). But if you are interested in the history of the island, I'd suggest the lower route (LP2 signposted to Los Canarios). This runs via El Hoyo de Mazo (10km ✗). Souvenir hunters may enjoy El Molino, the hillside windmill and ceramics shop on the outskirts of El Hoyo (11km), which was originally an ironmongery. It is beautifully kept, and in spring the garden is an extravaganza of colour. The artisans here specialise in replicas of the Guanche era. Further on you would pass the Cueva de Belmaco★ (15.5km ∩M), a large overhang of rock by the roadside with an archaeological museum. Four rocks on the edge of the overhang are engraved with still-undeciphered whorl-shaped petroglyphs.

Continuing the main tour uphill on the LP206, keep left at both the junctions you encounter and ignore any turn-offs. The garden plots disappear and the hillsides are overgrown. Entering **Mazo** (11.5km ╬▲✕⊕ and Las Toscas ⌂), take the upper road. The market and handicraft centre here are popular with tourists, as is the Corpus Christi festival in June, when flower petals are laid in the streets. Mazo, like El Hoyo de Mazo, is a wine-producing area, well known for its strong red wine. Alternative Walk 7 ends here.

Beyond **Tigalate** (19km), the historians and shoppers rejoin the route at the Mazo/Los Canarios junction. The LP2 takes you across a jagged lava stream, dating from the 1646 eruption of Volcán Martín (Walk 9). A few roadside picnic tables and benches lie along the route (⌂), and at the 25km-mark a track turns off right to the Fuente de los Roques *zona recreativa*.

Soon the change in scenery is spectacular. Volcanoes begin appearing on the southern tip of the island, where eruptions have dramatically transformed the landscape. Pines are liberally dispersed across the lava, which is covered in reindeer moss. The *cumbre* falls into the sea. Entering the wine-producing village of **Los Canarios** (formerly know as Fuencaliente; 28km ▲✕🚲⊕), where Walk 9 ends and Walk 8 begins, you pass the turn-offs for both the lighthouse (Faro de Fuencaliente) and the volcanoes. The village, the highest on the island, sits on the tail of the *cumbre*, at 680m/2230ft. If you're ready for coffee, try the almond cakes in the Bar La Parada, along to the right. Otherwise, take the turning left alongside Restaurant Parilla Grill (good local meat and fish dishes). Keep straight downhill, then turn right along the road to Las Indias and the volcanoes of San Antonio and Teneguía. This is one of the best grape-growing areas in the Canaries, and soon you will see the large Bodega Llanovid (also known as Bodega Teneguía; ✕) on your right. This bodega is known for its large selection of wines, the most famous being the well-known *malvasia* (malmsey).

Descending into the volcanic world that is the setting for Walk 8, weird and wonderful sights await you. Less than 1km downhill, turn left on a signposted gravel road for the **Volcán de San Antonio**★ (29.5km; paid parking and visitor centre; *i*🏠). Thought to be at least 3200 years old, it last erupted in 1677. (See Walk 8 on pages 73-74 to reach **Roque Teneguía** and the **Volcán de Teneguía**★ from here.)

Continuing towards Las Indias, you have a fine view (📷) onto yellow Roque Teneguía, once a sacred rock, covered with petroglyphs, with the rich blue sea behind it. The jet-black inclines are splashed with lime-green grape vines. Banana plantations lie along the sea flat amidst the lava flows. The village of Los Quemados sits on a pause in the hillside below. Ignore the turn-offs to the left. Descending through the sprawling hillside village of **Las Indias** (33km), you look across the southern slopes onto Puerto Naos, with the wall of the *caldera* behind it. Following signs for 'La Zamora' and 'El Faro', you come to a T-junction where you turn left. (Or first take a 4km return detour to the *right,* to the pretty little coves of Playa de Zamora and Playa Chica. Some 200m past the signposted track down to the parking area for Playa Chica, you'll see a path descending to Playa de Zamora, a cove set at the foot of high cliffs. Please don't sit directly below the cliffs, as there is often rockfall. Several rocky islets sit offshore, and the coastline has pinkish cliffs.)

Turning left at the bottom of the road, you weave in and out of banana plantations and pass an impressive hotel complex. A pretty inlet follows some 2km further on. Just afterwards a track turns off to the right, to the weekend retreat of Punta Larga (I highly recommend its seafood restaurant). Out of the banana groves, you head through old and newer lava flows. The newer flow was caused by Teneguía in 1971 and embraces the pretty beach of Playa Echentive (or Playa Nueva; 43.5km). Some 1km further on, turn right for 'El Faro'. Keep right at the fork. (The left fork would take you to some tiny unfrequented coves hidden in the shoreline, worth a visit one day.) **Faro de Fuencaliente** (45.5km ✖; photographs pages 76-77), the out-of-the-way fishermen's retreat where Walk 8 ends, is well worth the visit. There is a small but interesting maritime visitors' centre in the lighthouse. The reasonably-priced, no-frills restaurant here is always packed out with hikers. This is

The Volcán de Teneguía: in summer the nearby vineyards are a blaze of brightness in this sombre and windswept landscape.

also a good swimming spot, except when a strong south or southwesterly wind is blowing. The public may enter the salt pans here, but you must keep to the walkways.

Return to the road and turn right. The deep red-tinted Volcán de Teneguía catches your attention as you ascend into volcanic mounds. A steep climb through the fresh lava streams of Teneguía takes you back up to Los Canarios (57km), and you pass through the apron of vineyards that encircle the village. Back on the LP2, turn left, soon passing a roadside picnic area (⊼) overlooking the coast. Half a kilometre further along lies the **Mirador de las Indias** (📷), from where you have an excellent view back over terraced vineyards and the village of the same name. The road climbs to 800m/2625ft, with marvellous sea views. At 63.5km another *mirador* (📷) affords fine views across the cliffs, over to Puerto Naos. Beyond a shady pine wood, you overlook great spewings of lava from eruptions in the 18th century. The picturesque village of **Jedey** sits amidst this turmoil. **Las Manchas**, an area of viticulture, follows. Then you come to one of the most popular bodegas on the island, Bodega/Restaurant Tamanca (71km ✕), a cave cut into the hillside. At the very least try some cheese and ham with a tipple! You'll see the mounted head of a moufflon in the bar: a few still roam the heights of the *caldera*.

The village of **San Nicolás** lies just around the bend. During the volcanic eruption of 1949, San Nicolás was in the path of a descending lava flow. The people prayed together to save their village, and the flow changed course. It encircled the village, but then continued below it. A chapel commemorates this miracle.

Remain on the LP2 beyond San Nicolás. Settlement slowly creeps over the sloping plain. On reaching the Los Canarios/Los Llanos junction, at **Tajuya** (76km ✕), turn right uphill on the LP3 to El Paso. The towering crater walls are the focal point in the landscape. **El Paso** (79km ✝ ▲▲ ▲ ✕ ⊡ ⊕) sprawls amidst the gardens, orchards, and almond fields that cover the floor of a high open valley. This village is a favourite with expatriates.

Some 3km above El Paso, at a junction (▲✕ and *i*: National Park Information Centre), turn left on the LP302 for the Parque Nacional. Pass through the first junction (where a right turn leads to the Ermita de la Virgen del Pino and a grand pine; *P*6, Walk 6), then keep right at the next junction for La Cumbrecita. (Keeping straight on here would take you to the starting point for Walk 10 which climbs Pico Bejenado.) From the **Mirador Punta de los Roques** at **La Cumbrecita** (89km 📷) you enjoy a splendid view over the Caldera de Taburiente, a massive cauldron filled with jagged blades of tumbling ridges.

Return to the LP3 and turn left. After 3km turn right on the LP301 for the Zona Recreativa El Pilar and climb steadily, in an appealing landscape of coal-black slopes and pine forest. You pass a track off right 4km uphill: it leads to the small volcanic 'desert' shown on page 67, the Llano del Jable (📷 *P*7c, Walk 7). Crossing the *cumbre*, you pass the **Refugio El Pilar** (106km △ ⋒ *P*7b, Walks 6,

7 and 9), a popular picnic and camping area in a pine forest. Just above it, to the left, is the Cumbre Nueva track that is followed in Alternative walk 6-1.

On the other side of the *cumbre* the vegetation changes from pines to heather. A dark green carpet of dense woods stretches across the eastern escarpment. This fine view reaches as far as Puntallana. On clear days El Teide can be seen above the foaming white clouds that separate La Palma and Tenerife (☞ at 109km). Some 1.5km below the viewpoint lies **La Pared Vieja** (⌂*P*7a, Walk 7), a picnic area in laurel woods.

Returning to civilisation, you enter the farming village of **San Isidro** (118km), which enjoys an expansive panorama along the wall of the *cumbre* and over the twin villages of San Pedro and San José. San Isidro is known for its cattle market, held in May. Continuing downhill, soon you'll spot a large dragon tree below the road, off a sharp bend — actually two trees, intertwined (**Los Dragos Gemelos★**; the 'twins'). Reaching the LP202, head left into **San Pedro** (also known as Breña Alta; 123km ♠✕🖵) in the midst of a tobacco-growing area. Circle the *plaza*, remaining on the LP202. At the next important junction, cross the LP3, to continue towards the 'Santuario de las Nieves'. But first turn off right just beyond the junction, to the **Mirador de la Concepción** (☞), the perfect spot from which to view Santa Cruz. Back at the turn-off, keep straight on across the LP202. You pass the island's most famous restaurant, Chipi Chipi, on the left. Reasonably-priced and housed in cabanas in a courtyard crammed with greenery, it is always packed.

Rounding a bend, you look across a ravine sprinkled with palms to the tree-shaded **Santuario de las Nieves★** (129km ✝M), strikingly set in a rocky ridge. The church (16C) houses a 15th-century terracotta statue of the island's patron saint, Our Lady of the Snows. Her festival is celebrated annually on the fifth of August. But every five years a month-long fiesta takes place (the 'Bajada de la Virgen'), when the statue is carried down into Santa Cruz. It draws tens of thousands of pilgrims and tourists.

Now following signs for Santa Cruz, take the second turning to the right. A very steep, winding descent takes you back to **Santa Cruz** far below (134km).

Los Llanos • Caldera de Taburiente • Barranco de las Angustias • Los Brecitos • Tazacorte • Mirador El Time • (Puntagorda) • Los Llanos

60km/37mi; 3-4h driving. See also large-scale map on pages 88-89.

On route: Picnic (see pages 7-10) 11; Walks 11, 12. (Walks 13 and 14 and the El Fayal picnic site (🍴) are on the Puntagorda detour route.)

This tour should only be made in a 4WD vehicle, because of the rough track up to Los Brecitos (the route is also vertiginous). Parking is no longer allowed at Los Brecitos, so you may be turned back by a park warden if there are too many cars. The best solution is to drive only as far as the Barranco de las Angustias, the floor of the crater, and then take one of the shuttle jeep or van taxis up to Los Brecitos (these only operate from 08.30 until about 12.30); the shared cost is about 10 €.

A ll visitors to La Palma should spend at least one day in the magnificent Caldera de Taburiente. This short tour is designed to be combined with Shorter walk 11, as a half-day tour, half-day hike.

Leaving from **Los Llanos** (✝🏨🛏️✕🖥️⊕), turn north on Avenida Doctor Fleming and turn right at the T-junction. The road curves round to the left: go through an intersection and follow signs for 'La Caldera', keeping right at the first fork and left at the second. Climb to the edge of the Barranco de las Angustias and, at a junction, turn right to descend into the **Caldera de Taburiente★**. Less than 6km along you're in the bed of the dramatic **Barranco de las Angustias** (*P*11); see notes for Walk 11 on page 86 to make the most of your visit. If you will be doing Shorter walk 11, take a jeep taxi up to Los Brecitos *now* — they only run in the morning.

If there are not too many tourists about, and the park wardens don't turn you back, you may be able to take your 4WD further up the track. Whether with your own wheels or by jeep taxi, the 11km climb of almost 1000m/ 3300ft, through mountain scenery unequalled on the island, takes you to **Los Brecitos** (17km 📷), where Shorter walk 11 begins and ends.

From the *caldera* retrace your route to **Los Llanos** (34km) and turn right on the main LP2. Some 2km downhill, follow the LP2 left to **Tazacorte**

On the climb to Los Brecitos

(39.5km 🔺🔺🔺✕🚰⊕), buried amidst the banana plantations that cover these slopes. Continue through the village to **Puerto de Tazacorte** (42km 🔺✕), a colourful and fashionable seaside village with lovely restaurants lining the boulevard beside the beach. From here ascend the canyon-sized Barranco de las Angustias again (photograph page 94). Joining the LP1, continue left uphill to the **Mirador El Time** (49.5km 📷✕), the climax of one of the island's most exhilarating routes. The impressive *barranco* plunges 500m/1650ft directly below you here, and your view fans out over the banana plantations that fill the extensive Los Llanos valley, to the *cumbre,* and along the volcano-dented southern spine. Walk 12 winds its way down these sheer cliffs to Puerto de Tazacorte; it makes an excellent late afternoon walk.

Suggested detour, 32km return: If you have time, consider going on to Puntagorda via Tijarafe (✕🚰⊕) and Tinizara (✕). Tijarafe's Walk 13, which will turn your legs to jelly, is a must for the fit. Walk 14 is a gentler roller-coaster hike, from Tijarafe to Tinizara. At Puntagorda there is the El Fayal picnic site and a nearby indoor market selling local foods and handicrafts (weekends only)

Otherwise, pour yourself a glass of the local wine, put your feet up, and take in an 'El Time sunset', before heading back the 9.5km along the LP1 to **Los Llanos** (60km).

4 EL HIERRO — THE ISLAND'S HIGHLIGHTS

Tigaday • Sabinosa • La Dehesa • (Faro de Orchilla) • Cruz de los Reyes • Hoya del Morcillo • El Pinar • Cala de Tacorón • Mirador de las Playas • Mirador de Jinama • Mirador de la Peña • Mocanal • Pozo de las Calcosas • Valverde • San Andrés • Tigaday

184km/115mi; 5h driving; start out from Tigaday.

On route: ⏍ at Playa del Verodal, (Laja de Orchilla), Hoya del Morcillo, Cala de Tacorón; Picnics (see pages 7-10) 18a-b, 19, 20; Walks 17-20

This tour follows roads of all kinds. Some 25km is on gravel (not recommended immediately after wet weather, due to rockfall). The detour to the Faro de Orchilla takes in an extra 9km of sometimes rough road (in winter or after heavy rain only suitable for four wheel drive vehicles). There are two narrow stretches of road without guard rails which some motorists may find unnerving: on the ascent up the cumbre beyond the turn-off to Playa del Verodal, and on the road to the Cala de Tacorón in the south. Note that visibility on the cumbre can be zero, due to low clouds and mist. Always be alert for foraging animals. Petrol is only available at Taibique (near El Pinar), Tigaday and Valverde. All the roads are generally narrow and winding, so drive slowly.

Opening hours
Eco-museo de Guinea: *In winter* 10.00-14.00 and 16.00-18.00 Tue-Sat; 11.00-14.00 Sun. *In summer* 10.30-14.30 and 17.00-19.00 Tue-Sat
Lagartario: *In winter* 10.00-14.00 and 16.00-18.00 Tue, Thur, Sat. *In summer* 10.30-14.30 and 17.00-19.00 Tue, Wed, Thur, Sat

The diversity of landscapes encountered on this tiny island will leave you spellbound. There are vast open tracts of lava, fields of craters, herbaceous highlands, spacious forests of towering pines, small boskets of laurel, and inviting rock pools. If you're rushed for time, then keep to the main tour, but if you're on the island for a few days, then *do* try to take all the suggested detours.

Tigaday is the starting point for the drive. For those of you staying elsewhere, recommended sights in the vicinity are the Eco-museo de Guinea, a restored hamlet, and the nearby Lagartario which houses the large Salmor lizards (both on the road to Las Puntas); the Embarcadero de Punta Grande (if only to see the smallest hotel in the world!); and the bell-tower of Frontera's church, which crowns a rust-red volcanic hill above the church itself. The hilltop is the perfect spot to take in a sunset.

Set out from **Frontera/Tigaday** (♦️🏔🔺✕🛒⊕) by heading west towards Sabinosa on the HI50. You pass through a string of villages (✕) set on the steep rocky volcanic slopes that roll down off the *cumbre*. Fig trees and vineyards grow out of the *malpais* that coats the slopes (try the fine local wine, the *vino de pata*).

Rounding a hillside, you overlook **Sabinosa** (8km 🔺✕), the village shown on page 114. Stark and severe, this whitewashed settlement is the island's prize — superbly sited on volcanic slopes at the foot of the wooded central spine of mountains. Short walk 17-2 starts here, and Short walk 17-1 ends here. Terraced vineyards ladder the surrounding hillsides.

A narrow winding road takes you down to the health spa of **Pozo de la Salud**★ (12km 🏔🔺✕📷), known for the reputedly curative powers of its sulphur and radium spring. This one-horse hamlet enjoys a superb backdrop. From the pretty, manicured *mirador* below the hotel you can look along the low craggy sea cliffs into a viridescent sea. Drink some of the salty spring water from the little well in the rock here, where the sheer *cumbre* walls provide a magnificent backdrop; the scenery alone has curative powers!

Continuing further west, you enter the island's most striking and isolated corner, where an extravaganza of volcanic scenery awaits you. Shortly you spot Arenas Blancas, a tiny patch of white sand set in the lava coastline. Disappearing into *malpais* again, stabs of rich volcanic reds and orange-tinted rust-brown hues catch your attention. Your next turn-off comes up at 17.5km: turn sharp

Looking across Tigaday and Frontera to the wall of the El Golfo crater. The bell-tower of Frontera's church (Virgen de la Candelaria) stands apart on a rust-red hilltop. Walk 18 ascends the wooded slopes at the right-hand side of the photograph.

right for 'Playa del Verodal' and take the second turning right off this rough track. The red sandy beach of **Playa del Verodal** (18.5km ⊼) is a pretty, but windy spot, with a dramatic backdrop of maroon-tinted cliffs. *Beware:* the sea can be rough here!

Back on the main road, turn right. Ascending steeply, superb views over the coastal lava shelf unfold behind you. The landscape is barren and rocky; xerophytic vegetation grows out of the rock. This part of the island is known as **La Dehesa**.

Suggested detour: Some 27km en route you reach the signposted turn-off right for the Faro de Orchilla. The first 2km is partly asphalted, then you turn left on a motorable track (in winter or after heavy rain only suitable for 4WD). Descending to the lighthouse, you enter a world of volcanic cones and lava streams and look down over a jagged, lava-encrusted point of land. Notice the massive *Euphorbias* growing out of the lava here. Red-tinted craters come out of hiding. Approaching the lighthouse, you pass a fork leading left to the tiny port at Laja de Orchilla (⊼), where it's possible to swim. Up until 1844, the Faro de Orchilla★ (📷) was 'the edge of the world': before it was repositioned at Greenwich, 0° of longitude was located here at the western edge of El Hierro. Amble along the impressive sea cliffs behind the building. Then return to the main road and turn right to continue the tour.

The main tour bypasses the Orchilla turn-off. You drive over two cattle-grids and, at the junction that follows, turn left for the 'Mirador del Basco' and 'El Sabinar', soon coming to the **Ermita de la Virgen de los Reyes★** (30.5km ✝; Walk 17). This dazzling-white, isolated refuge (photograph page 111) is the sanctuary of the island's patron saint. Every four years, on the first weekend in July, a very popular pilgrimage (the 'Bajada de la Virgen') begins here, and an image of the Madonna crosses the island to Valverde.* The fiesta continues for almost a month.

Half a kilometre further on the way reverts to a rutted gravel road. At a signposted junction, turn left. Another cattle-grid is encountered, and again the countryside changes. Undulating pastures criss-crossed with stone walls stretch back up to the hills. Remaining on the main metalled road, take the first turn-off left and wind your

---

*The island's most famous walk, the 28km-long 'Camino de la Virgin', follows this pilgrimage route; a leaflet detailing the various stages is available from tourist offices. It is also shown on our walking maps, since we follow the trail from time to time.

The Eco-museo de Guinea near Tigaday — a restored old village. Right: Hotel at Pozo de la Salud, with the cliffs of the cumbre rising vertically in the background.

way down to **El Sabinar★** (34.5km), a magnificent refuge for scatterings of centuries-old, twisted and gnarled *sabinas* (native junipers) — the result, I assume, of the harsh unrelenting winds that batter this corner of the island. Less than 1km downhill, the track ends just in front of the island's most famous and most photographed specimen (see page 1). These 'arthritic' trees are unique in the archipelago. The surrounding vegetation here is thickly covered in moss and lichen. Please note that this is a protected area.

Return to the junction and turn left. Further north along the gravel road, you meet a fork: keep right for the *mirador,* driving through fragments of pine woods — a picturesque corner in this inhospitable area. The **Mirador del Basco** (36.5km 📷) sits high on the very edge of the escarpment that encircles El Golfo. The stunning panorama extends all across the gulf, with Pozo de la Salud immediately below you.

Returning to the junction just before the *ermita* (41km),

turn left. A meandering ascent takes you up to the island's cloud-swept heights. Pines patch the gravelly slopes. Pass the turn-off right for El Julán and Hoya del Morcillo, and keep left, now on a gravel road. Volcanic hues of maroon, pink, and yellow stain the hillsides. High on the *cumbre,* your view stretches over the pines to the sea and then to the treeless southern tip of La Restinga. You pass below El Hierro's highest summit, Malpaso (1500m/4920ft), without even noticing it.

A simple wooden cross and concrete altar by the side

Rock pools (charcos) *at Cala de Tacorón*

of the road mark **Cruz de los Reyes** (56.5km), the pilgrims' rest stop en route to Valverde from the Ermita de la Virgen de los Reyes. On a sealed road once again, you look out over the low wooded hills of El Pinar, your next destination. Coming to the Frontera/Valverde junction (starting point for Walk 20), keep right along the HI1, immediately passing the starting point for Walk 19 and the signposted path to the **Mirador de la Llanía** (📷*P*19). Some 0.4km further on, turn right for 'Hoya del Morcillo, El Pinar, La Restinga'. Briefly disappearing into laurel woods, the road winds down towards El Pinar, passing through El Hierro's majestic Canary pine wood, where centuries-old pines with massive girths leave you in awe. Just under 4km downhill, keep right. Follow this up with a left turn into the large picnic area of **Hoya del Morcillo** (64.5km △🆔), set in the middle of the forest. Return to the main road and turn right for El Pinar and La Restinga. At the T-junction that follows, turn right again. The nearby slopes are liberally sprinkled with almond trees.

Entering **El Pinar**, which comprises the villages of **Las Casas** and **Taibique**, take the first right turn (signposted 'Tanajara'), where the main road curves left. Keep straight through a junction, then turn right at the next junction and ascend a narrow road up to the **Mirador Tanajara** (69km 📷). If you're game, climb the rickety old viewing platform for a good view over the sprawling villages of Las Casas and Taibique. The fields are scattered with large umbrella-shaped fig trees, and almond, apricot and pear trees abound, as do small vineyards. To the south lies a chain of volcanic craters. Back on the main road, descend to **Taibique** (72.5km 🏨🛏️✕🚌⊕M). The village is known for its handicrafts: woodcarving, basketry, and weaving.

Out of the village, you descend south through a curious landscape of ropey lava and block lava. Less than 10km below El Pinar, turn off right for Cala de Tacorón (signposted). Descending into a striking sea view across the western wing of the island, the road twists its way down a sheer slope to a lava platform jutting out into the sea. **Cala de Tacorón** (87km 🆔) is a quiet, out-of-the-way spot with superb *charcos* (sea pools) for swimmers and mouth-watering scenery. With the south's more reliable sunshine, this is the place to come for your beach day. It beats La Restinga hands down. The main tour in fact bypasses La Restinga (🛏️✕), by turning left at the Tacorón junction, heading straight back to El Pinar. (La Restinga, small fishing village-cum-resort, 7km to the south, has little to offer other than good fish restaurants.)

From **El Pinar** keep straight uphill past the El Morcillo junction, then turn off right to the **Mirador de las Playas** (109.5km 📷; Walk 20). From the edge of a 1000m/ 3300ft-high bluff, you look straight down onto the severe but breathtakingly beautiful *playas* — the setting shown in the photograph on page 126.

Back on the main road, head right. The hillsides are covered in *tagasaste,* a shrub grown for animal fodder. Climbing to a tableland, you reach the roof of the island, home of the best pastures, where cows and sheep graze. San Andrés is the small village over on the right, encircling the base of a small volcanic cone (photograph page 127). When you rejoin the HI1, keep left and, 2km along, turn right to the **Mirador de Jinama** (117.5km 📷; *P*18a, Walk 18) where, from the top of the *cumbre*, your view stretches the length of El Golfo to the west.

Continuing northeast on a narrow country road, bump your way across the plateau, lost amidst the myriad of stone walls that divide it up into tiny squares. When a farmer dies on El Hierro, his fields are always divided up among all his children, each of whom partitions his or her share. And so the fields get smaller, while the walls increase. Small cinder cones cover the plateau.

You descend to the HI10, where you turn left downhill for 2km to the **Mirador de la Peña★** (124.5km 📷✕; *P*18b, Walk 18). Lanzarote's César Manrique was the creator of this superbly-sited restaurant/ bar, which claims the island's best view of El Golfo. These cliffs were the habitat of a very rare lizard, the *lagarto de salmor,* which supposedly reaches a length of 70cm/28in. (*Do* visit the Lagartario at the Eco-museo de Guinea!)

Continuing north through fertile farmlands and the hamlets of **Guarazoca** and **Erese**, dense xerophytic vegetation cloaks the rocky inclines. The traditional stone dwellings are hardly noticeable in this backdrop. Entering **Mocanal** (128km), the most picturesque village on the island, take the first turn-off left (along the old road). This narrow road squeezes past a string of charming old houses, where window and door frames all vary in colour.

Just over 1km along, at a T-junction, turn left for Pozo de las Calcosas. A steep winding descent follows. The slopes ease out as they roll seawards. *Vinagrera* (of the dock family) proliferates here and provides a source of food for the many goats. ('Calcosas' is the local name for *vinagrera.*) At a fork, keep left for **Pozo de las Calcosas**★ (133.5km ▲✕🎞), which at first appears to be an unexciting hamlet set back off the sea cliffs. However, on the rocky shore at the foot of these bluffs sits a century-old, once-deserted fishing hamlet which has been beautifully restored. Steps lead down to this appealing huddle of stone houses and the nearby natural rock pool. The restaurants above the *mirador* here serve excellent fresh seafood.

At the junction above Pozo de las Calcosas, turn left for **Echedo** (138.5km ✕), a wine- and fruit-producing village boasting the best climate on the island. Entering the village, ignore a turning to the right, but turn right at the T-junction that follows. (A left turn at this T-junction would take you to the brilliant blue sea pools of Charco Manso, 4km away.) Surrounded by rocky hills and scattered amidst the now-familiar stone walls, Echedo is a charmer. Ascending to Valverde, you overlook the black and brown slopes of Montaña Tanagiscaba. Meet the main road and turn left.

Just beyond the **Mirador de las Pernadas** (🎞), from where there is a fine view over the tiny seaside resort of Tamaduste, you come to a junction on the outskirts of **Valverde** (142km ✝▲▲▲✕🖳⊕M). This small, rather plain rural town sits at an altitude of 700m. Turn right and pass through the town. There's little of interest here.

Suggested detours: If you are on the island for a while, you may wish to visit the seaside resort of Tamaduste (▲✕), 8km north of the capital via the airport road, or take the very scenic coastal route from Puerto de la Estaca (two ⊼) to the *parador* (▲▲ ✕), 18km southeast of Valverde.

Leave Valverde on the HI1. Bypassing Tiñor, you climb above steep, rocky, xerophyte-clad slopes to the small traditional farming village of **San Andrés** (✕). At an altitude of 1100m, this is El Hierro's highest village. (The turn-off to Isora, just before San Andrés, leads to the Mirador de Isora, another spectacular lookout point over Las Playas. Alternative walk 20 makes a fairly hair-raising descent down the sheer escarpment that tumbles away below this *mirador*.) The famous 'Arbol Santo' worshipped by the Bimbaches (El Hierro's original inhabitants) is not far from San Andrés; Walk 20 would take you to it.

Go straight through both junctions just outside San Andrés, and once again weave your way through the maze of stone walls, following the HI1 back to **Tigaday** (175km).

✻ Walking

La Palma and El Hierro offer unlimited scope for walkers. This book covers a good cross-section of walks on both islands. Due to the rugged, mountainous terrain of these islands, many of the walks in the book are quite strenuous, but I usually suggest a less difficult alternative — perhaps a short walk, or just a stroll to a picnic spot.

G uides, waymarking, maps

Should you wish to hire a **guide**, enquire at the tourist offices or the national hotels (*paradores*).

A great many trails on **La Palma** are now **waymarked** and signposted (but that doesn't necessarily mean that they are in good condition or suitable for inexperienced walkers!). There are three types of waymarking:

- *Red and white* waymarks indicate GR routes ('Grandes Recorridos': long-distance footpaths);
- *Yellow and white* waymarks indicate PR routes ('Pequeños Recorridos': short trails of up to six hours);
- *Green and white* waymarks indicate SL routes ('Senderos Locales': local trails, up to about 10km long).
- For all these routes, right-angled stripes indicate a 'change of direction; an 'X' means 'wrong way'.

We have shown the *approximate* line of these way-marked routes and their numbers *in purple* on our walking maps. *This should give you ample scope for devising even more walks — whether you want a linear route to catch a bus or a short-cut back to your car.* Ask for the overview map 'Hiking paths of La Palma' at tourist offices, to see the whole network of waymarked trails.

While paths on **El Hierro** are not yet fully waymarked, they *are* well signposted. Again we have shown some established routes on our maps with purple dashes.

The **maps** in this book, based on Spanish military maps and reproduced at a scale of 1:50,000, cover most of both islands and have been heavily adapted and updated. If you require further maps, you should find the Freytag + Berndt maps of La Palma (1:50,000) and El Hierro (1:30,000) more useful than the older military maps.

W here to stay

There are two main resorts on **La Palma**: Los Cancajos on the eastern side of the island and Puerto Naos on the western side. Both are fairly well served by public transport. But I would recommend Santa Cruz or Los Llanos over either of these resorts, both for atmosphere and for getting to and from walks by public transport. If you have a hire car, however, the island's your oyster — and you might choose to rent one of the *casas rurales.* These are charming old country houses converted into tourist accommodation. They are reasonably priced and often superbly located. *I highly recommend them.* For information, contact the Asociación de Turismo Rural (tel: 922-430625; fax: 922-430308) or surf the web: www.ecoturismocanarias.com.

The main tourist centres on **El Hierro** are Tigaday/ Frontera and La Restinga. Tigaday is my choice, but La Restinga boasts more sunshine. Although bus services on the island have increased somewhat, you really *do* need to rent a car to make the best of El Hierro.

Both La Palma and El Hierro have **government-run hotels** *(paradores).* El Hierro's is magnificently sited (see photograph on page 126), but well off the beaten track. Independent travellers should always book their accommodation a few nights in advance — in the peak season (Christmas through Easter), at least a month in advance!

Transport
The public transport network on La Palma is good enough for you to be able to do most of the walks I describe using the local buses. However, on El Hierro, there is only one bus a day from the outlying villages to the capital (Valverde), so you will often have to use a taxi.

What to take
If you've come to the islands without special equipment, you can still do many of the walks — or you can buy the basic equipment at one of the sports shops. *Don't* attempt the more difficult walks without the proper gear. For each walk, the *minimum year-round* equipment is listed. Above all, you need strong shoes or boots with *ankle support.* You may find this checklist useful:

stout shoes or walking boots	long trousers, tight at the ankles
waterproof rain gear (outside summer months)	insect repellent
	knives and openers
long-sleeved shirt (sun protection)	light cardigans (or similar)
bandages and plasters, tissues	extra pair of (long) socks
water bottle, plastic plates, etc	whistle, torch, compass
anorak (zip opening)	antiseptic cream
sunhat, sunglasses, suncream	small rucksack
spare bootlaces	plastic groundsheet
jacket or woollen shirt	up-to-date bus timetables
gloves	bathing suit, etc

Weather

The average yearly temperature on both islands is 20°C — perfect for hiking. Three chief winds determine the weather on both islands. The **trade wind** (*el alisio*) comes from the **northeast** with speeds of anything up to 25km/h. Its low, fluffy clouds hover over the north for much of the year, lying at a height of 600-1500m (2000-5000ft). They bring lots of moisture and so keep the islands green. However, the southern sides of the islands are much drier and hotter. The *tiempo del sur* is an **easterly or southeasterly** wind which originates over the Sahara and brings hot weather, usually accompanied by fine dust particles. Between November and March, **northwesterly and southwesterly** winds may blow in with storms. Seldom will this ruin an entire day, *but never venture into the mountains when a strong wind is blowing from the west; it's far too dangerous!*

Dogs — and other nuisances

The few **dogs** you'll encounter are mostly all bark, no bite. But if dogs worry you, you might like to invest in a 'Dog Dazer' — an ultrasonic device which persuades aggressive dogs to back off without harming them. These are available from Sunflower Books: contact them for more information (www.sunflowerbooks.co.uk).

Ticks *are* a nuisance: they're prevalent in spring. Keep arms and legs covered, and the problem is solved. On El Hierro, if you're crossing pastures, give **billy goats** a wide berth, and make sure there's a wall/fence between you and the **bulls**! During the hunting season, **hunters** blasting away may frighten you. Exercise your lungs if you think they're too close. Neither island has any snakes. Black widow **spiders** are found on both islands, and also red or black **centipedes**, which also have a dangerous sting.

Country code for walkers and motorists

The experienced rambler is used to following a 'country code', but the tourist out for a lark may unwittingly cause damage, harm animals, and even endanger his own life. Do heed this advice:

- **Do not light fires.** Stub out cigarettes with care.
- **Do not frighten animals.** The goats and sheep you may encounter on your walks are not tame. By making loud noises or trying to touch or photograph them, you may cause them to run in fear and be hurt.
- **Take all your litter away with you.**

- **Walk quietly** through all farms, hamlets and villages, *leaving all gates as you found them.*

- **Protect all wild and cultivated plants.** Don't try to pick wild flowers or uproot saplings. Obviously fruit and crops are someone's private property and should not be touched. *Never walk over cultivated land.*

- **Walkers: do not take risks!** Do not attempt walks beyond your capacity and **never walk alone.** *Always* tell a responsible person *exactly* where you are going and what time you plan to return. Heed this advice, and there will be no cause for panic in an emergency:
  — **at any time a walk may become unsafe** due to storm damage or the havoc caused by bulldozers. If the route is not as described in this book, and your way ahead is not secure, *turn back;*
  — **strenuous walks** are unsuitable in high summer;
  — **mountain walks** are unsuitable in wet or very windy weather;
  — **do not overestimate your energies**: your speed will be determined by the slowest walker in the group;
  — **four people** comprise the best walking group. If someone is injured, two people can go for help;
  — **transport connections** at the end of the walk may be vital;
  — **proper shoes or boots** are a necessity;
  — **warm clothing** is needed in the mountains, *even in summer;*
  — **extra food and drink** should be taken on long walks;
  — **always take a sunhat** and cover arms and legs as well;
  — **compass, torch, whistle, first-aid kit** weigh little, but might save your life.

Spanish for walkers

English is not widely spoken on La Palma, and few people on El Hierro speak it at all. Try to learn a few words of Spanish: although the inhabitants are reserved towards foreigners, they *will* respond warmly to spoken Spanish.

Here's an (almost) foolproof way to communicate in Spanish. First, memorise the few short key questions and their possible answers, given below. Then, when you have your 'mini-speech' memorised, always ask the many questions you can concoct from it **in such a way that you get a 'sí' (yes) or 'no' answer.** Never ask an open-ended question such as 'Where is the main road?' Instead, ask the question and then *suggest the most likely answer* *yourself.* For instance: 'Good day, sir. Please — where is the path to Los Tilos? *Is it straight ahead?*' Now, unless you get a '*sí*' response, try: '*Is it to the left?*' If you go through the list of answers to your own question, you will eventually get a '*sí*' response ... more reassuring than relying solely on sign language.

Following are the two most likely situations in which you may have to practice your Spanish. The dots (...) show where you will fill in the name of your destination. Ask a native (someone at your hotel, a taxi driver) to help you with the pronunciation of place names.

■ Asking the way

The key questions

English	Spanish	pronounced as
Good day, sir (madam, miss)	Buenos días, señor (señora, señorita)	**Boo**-eh-nos **dee**-ahs, sen-**yor** (sen-**yor**-ah, sen-yor-**ee**-tah)
Please —	Por favor —	**Poor** fa-**vor** —
where is	dónde está	**dohn**-day es-**tah**
the road to ...?	la carretera a ...?	la cah-reh-**teh**-rah ah ...?
the footpath to ...?	la senda de ...?	lah **sen**-dah day ...?
the way to ...?	el camino a ...?	el cah-**mee**-noh ah ...?
the bus stop?	la parada?	lah par-**rah**-dah?
Many thanks.	Muchas gracias.	**Moo**-chas **gra**-thee-as.

Possible answers

English	Spanish	pronounced as
Is it here?	Está aquí?	Es-**tah** ah-**kee**?
straight ahead?	todo recto?	**toh**-doh **rec**-toh?
behind?	detrás?	day-**tras**?
to the right?	a la derecha?	ah lah day-**ray**-chah?
to the left?	a la izquierda?	ah lah eeth-kee-**er**-dah?
above?	arriba?	ah-**ree**-bah?
below?	abajo?	ah-**bah**-hoh?

■ Asking a taxi driver to take you somewhere and collect you later in the day

English	Spanish	pronounced as
Please	Por favor	**Poor** fah-**vor**
take us to ...	llévanos a ...	l-**yay**-vah-nos ah ...
and return	y volver	ee vol-**vair**
for us at ... (place)	para nosotros a ...	**pah**-rah nos-**oh**-tros ah ...
at ... (time)	a las ...	ah lahs ...

(Instead of memorising hours of the day, simply point out the time when you wish to return on your watch, and get his agreement.)

Organisation of the walks

The 16 main walks on La Palma are well dispersed across the island, with several being located near the centre. The four walks on El Hierro are located in the centre and north of the island.

I hope that the book is set out so that you can plan your

walks easily ... depending on how far you want to go, your abilities and equipment, and what time you are willing to get up in the morning! You might begin by considering the fold-out touring maps inside the back cover. Here you can see at a glance the overall terrain, the road network, and the general orientation of the walking maps in the text.

Quickly flipping through the book, you'll find that there is at least one photograph for every walk. Having selected one or two potential excursions from the map and photographs, look over the planning information at the beginning of each walk description. Here you'll find distance/walking time, grade, equipment, and how to get there by public transport (timetables begin on page 131). If the walk appears to be beyond your fitness or ability, see if a short or alternative version is given, which *does* appeal to you — or look at the map to see if a dashed purple line indicates a waymarked route (see page 36) that you could take as a short-cut back to your car. On hot days, the picnic strolls described on pages 7-10 may be as strenuous an adventure as you'd like to tackle.

When you are on your walk, you will find that the text begins with an introduction to the overall landscape and then quickly turns to a detailed description of the route itself.

Times are given for reaching certain points in the walk. *Important: do* compare your own times with those in the book on one or two short walks, before you set off on a long hike. Remember that I've included only *minimal stops* at viewpoints; allow ample extra time for photography, picnicking, or swimming. Don't forget to take **transport** connections into account!

The large-scale **maps** (all 1:50,000; see page 36) have been set out facing the walking notes if the route is isolated, but where several routes converge, they are often presented on facing pages, to help with overall orientation. Below is a key to the symbols on the maps:

▬▬▬	expressway	●▸	spring, tank, etc	■	specific building
▬▬▬	asphalt road	*P*	picnic suggestion	†	shrine or cross
▬▬▬	major track		(see pages 7-10)	✝ ↦	church.cemetery
▬▬	other track	▱	best views	☎	picnic site with
-------	path, steps	●	bus stop	굿	tables
₃₋→	main walk	⊟	car parking	⁝	danger! vertigo!
₃₋→	alternative walk	PR LP 9	*approximate* routes	▥	map continuation
		-------	of signposted trails*	*i*	visitor centre
▬▬	watercourse, pipe			☀ ∩	mill.cave
— 400 —	altitude (m)		*La Palma's trails are waymarked and numbered; see page 36.*	⩗	rock formation

1 FROM THE MIRADOR LA TOSCA TO GALLEGOS

Distance/time: 6km/3.7mi; 2h30min

Grade: moderate-strenuous, with total ascents of about 500m/1650ft. You must be sure-footed and have a head for heights. Not recommended in wet weather. *Red and white GR waymarking*

Equipment: walking boots, sunhat, sunglasses, suncream, raingear, long trousers, cardigan, anorak, picnic, water

How to get there: 🚌 from Santa Cruz (Línea 2) to the Barlovento terminus, then ongoing bus (same line) to the Mirador La Tosca; journey time about 1h20min — or walk from Barlovento to the start of the walk (about 15min). Or 🚗: park on the track where the walk begins.
To return: 🚌 from the Gallegos turn-off to Santa Cruz (Línea 2, via Barlovento) or the same bus line back to your car.

This is a roller-coaster walk. Crossing the isolated hills of the northeast, you dip into and out of *barrancos* all the way. But first, enjoy the stupendous view over the rugged north coast from the Mirador La Tosca (**P**1). It's a windswept landscape, where hamlets straggle down the dividing ridges; your hike will take you to Gallegos, the largest of these isolated outposts.

Start out at the **Mirador La Tosca**: walk back towards Barlovento along the main road (LP1). Take the first left turn (**7min**), along a concrete lane signposted 'GR130 — CAMINO REAL DE LA COSTA. GALLEGOS, GARAFÍA'. Three minutes downhill, turn left on a path (signposted 'CAMINO REAL DE GALLEGOS'), descending into the *barranco*. You cross the floor of the *barranco*, passing fallow plots concealed amidst the heather. Soon you round a bend, to enjoy a magnificent view to the distant sea-cliffs on the north coast (**15min**).

Coming onto a driveway in **La Tosca**, pass a house and bear left down to the village lane. Turn left up the lane. Meet another lane on a bend (SIGNPOST), and follow it to the right downhill. Two minutes later, the lane swings sharply right: turn left onto a concrete path (SIGNPOST), which soon reveals itself as the remains of the old cobbled *camino real*. If the *cumbre* is free of cloud, the white-domed observatory is visible.

Cross the floor of the **Barranco de Topaciegas**, choked with vegetation. After a steep climb up the far side, ignore paths left and right. Keep straight on until you meet a concrete lane (**40min**; SIGNPOST) and follow it uphill to the left. Leave the lane after 40m/yds, turning right on a sign-posted path. From here you have a good view of the *cumbre* with its seaward-tumbling ridges. Orchards and pockets of cultivation lie scattered across the landscape.

Dropping down into another, deeper *barranco* (**Barranco de la Vica**), your way is flanked by sticky *Cistus*. Just past the point where a path joins from the right, the way is vertiginous for a short stretch. Go through a couple of gates a minute apart (please leave them as you find them), and pass below an old goats' pen lying under a rock overhang.

Leaving the *barranco*, keep left at a fork, to come onto a concrete lane in **La Palmita (1h)**. Ascend the lane, cross over another lane, and pick up the signposted continuation of your *camino* some metres uphill. It drops you down into another *barranco*, this one full of blackberry bushes. On reaching a track, follow it to the right uphill. A minute later, at an intersection, keep straight on around the hillside. At the fork that follows, go right, downhill (SIGNPOST). Ignore minor tracks striking off left. Gallegos comes into view, looking deceptively close, but it's still two *barrancos* away.

Two minutes below the junction, the track veers right;

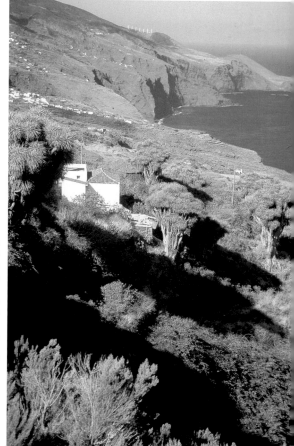

Over-looking the north of the island, with the village of La Tosca in the fore-ground (Picnic 1)

take the path on the left (SIGNPOST), into the penultimate *barranco*, the **Barranco de Gallegos**. It's the most impressive … and the most tiring! Winding down its vertical walls, you pass through two gates. The path is at times vertiginous and, nearer the bottom, the way might be overgrown. Cross the STREAM BED on boulders (**1h40min**). The climb out of this *barranco* is quite rough; goats have destroyed most of the path. Once out of the *barranco*, beyond another gate, you cross over a concrete lane which heads along the crest of the ridge (SIGNPOST). From here you have an excellent view of Gallegos, stepped down a declining rocky ridge. Now the path descends into the final ravine. Once in the bed of this *barranco*, where tethered sheep and goats graze, turn towards the sea to pick up your ongoing path out of the ravine.

Entering **Gallegos** (**2h**), you reach the main lane, opposite a bar. Having quenched your thirst, follow the street below the bar (a telephone box stands on the left). Keep straight on through the simple PLAZA DE LA FUENTE. Picture-postcard dwellings with colourful gardens lie hidden in the midst of vegetable plots, vineyards, orchards and banana groves. Completing the village circuit, climb straight up the hillside to join the lane serving the village, about 25 minutes uphill. The main road is a minute further uphill, and the BUS STOP is just opposite the village exit (**2h30min**).

2 LOS SAUCES • MIRADOR DE LAS BARANDAS • BARLOVENTO

Distance: 12km/7.5mi; 4h10min

Grade: strenuous, with an overall ascent of 900m/3000ft. The path out of the Barranco de Herradura, although secured, is steep, narrow and vertiginous. You must be sure-footed and have a head for heights. Don't attempt in wet weather. *Yellow and white PR waymarking along most of the walk*

Equipment: walking boots, sunhat, sunglasses, suncream, warm cardigan, raingear, picnic, plenty of water

How to get there: 🚌 from Santa Cruz to Los Sauces (Línea 2); journey time 50min. Or 🚗: park in Los Sauces.
To return: 🚌 from Barlovento to Santa Cruz (Línea 2); journey time about 1h20min. Or the same line to Los Sauces, to collect your car.

The north boasts the most impressive ravines on the island, amongst them the Barranco de Herradura — it's not to be missed. A forestry track leads you into this *barranco*, and a footpath not much wider than a pair of boots takes you back out of it. On the way in, you'll see magnificent colonies of La Palma's endemic blue *Echium* (viper's bugloss), a rival for Tenerife's *taginaste rojo* both in splendour and in height.

Begin the walk at the BUS STOP in **Los Sauces**. Cross the street and walk 10m/yds to the left. Then go uphill (at the right of a park), past the Ayuntamiento (town hall) and the pharmacy. Keep straight uphill, climbing steeply. This village has an authentic farmyard feel about it. Some of the old homes will take you by surprise with their unusually bright colours, while the gardens display a mixture of flowers, fruit trees and vegetables.

A renovated aqueduct on the left will catch your eye. The building here has been turned into a CENTRO DE ARTESANIA (**10min**). Just past the *centro,* turn right (signpost: PICO DE LA CRUZ, MIRADOR TOPO DE LA BARANDA, PR LP7). Not far uphill, the road forks. Both forks rejoin, but take the left fork — it's quicker. Once past the CAMPO DE FUTBOL, the climb steepens, as you rise through patchy cultivation. Soon after the forks have rejoined and the way has reverted to track, you reach the rim of **Barranco del Agua (30min)**, with an excellent view towards the *cumbre.*

From this lookout point, leave the track and climb a cobbled path to the left (SIGNPOST). Several minutes up, on rejoining the track (SIGNPOST), follow it to the left uphill. The steadily ascending track winds through scrub, a mixture of laurels, heather, ferns, *codeso (Adenocarpus),* and scatterings of old chestnut trees, while the Barranco de Herradura drops away to the right.

Ignore all turn-offs until you reach the turn-off left to the **Mirador de las Barandas** (**1h10min**). From the *mirador* you enjoy the splendid view shown opposite, looking straight down into the Barranco del Agua and across the heavily-wooded ridges that carve up the landscape.

Return the 120m/yds to the main track, to continue the walk. Ignore a first track off to the right but, 10 minutes from the *mirador,* fork right on a clear track (signpost: LAGUNA DE BARLOVENTO, PR LP7.1). Every now and then you'll see enormous viper's bugloss along the route. In summer their 4-5m/12-15ft-high stalks will be embellished with blue flowers. The native white-tailed and Bolle's laurel pigeons abound up here too. Ignore a track to the left.

Entering the **Barranco de Herradura**, the way becomes dark and shady. As you approach the valley floor, notice the caves cut into the bank on the left. A couple of minutes further along, the track ends at a concrete waterworks. You need to turn left 100m *before* the end of the track — on a faint but waymarked path. In just one minute you reach the **Galería Meleno** (**2h10min**). *Don't* enter the tunnel here, or you may be risking not only your own life, but that of the poor blighter who has to come and rescue you. An abandoned building stands on the left side of the ravine here, and some endemic geraniums grow beside the track.

The continuing path begins at the right of the abandoned building and is steep and vertiginous at the outset. A 'home-made' rickety wooden railing secures the path all the way, but don't trust it! The slopes are sheer, but wooded, thus lessening the exposure … at least psychologically. ***Important:*** *remember that the leaves covering the path are very slippery.* A good 10 minutes up, you round a bend and enter a shady mossy *barranco* with vertical walls; not only is this ravine so dark that it's difficult to appreciate its beauty, but your eyes *should* be glued to the path the whole time!

Close on 30 minutes up from the *barranco* floor, you rise to a CREST (**2h40min**; PR LP7.1 signpost). The path takes you to a track, soon flanked by garden plots. The Laguna de Barlovento (a large reservoir) appears through the trees, with a *zona recreativa* to its right. The surrounding hills are being cleared of trees and scrub to create gardens and orchards. Minutes out of the *barranco,* when you come to a T-junction, turn left (where a SIGNPOST points in the *opposite* direction). The *laguna* reappears not far ahead; later in the walk you will circle to the left of it.

Now ignore all side paths and tracks for the next 10 minutes, until you come to a major junction where a sign, 'Galería Adelfas', points in the direction from which you have come: turn right here. Now keep to the main track, ignoring all side tracks. Twenty minutes from the major junction, weave your way past a few buildings (visitors' centres and museums for a 'rural interpretation park' in the making), to join the road to the **Laguna de Barlovento** *zona recreativa* (**3h35min**). Turn left; then, some 50m/yds

The Barranco del Agua from the Mirador de las Barandas

along, leave the road: turn right on a track, heading into a cultivated basin. Ignore the fork to the right at the outset. Follow the same path/track, ignoring all turn-offs, until you reach the main road. Turn right for 100m/yds, then go left at the sign 'CAMPO DE FUTBOL'. When you reach the main road again, cross it and follow the track opposite. At a fork, take the path on the left. Cross the road and continue on the path, straight past cultivated fields and a housing estate. Reaching the main Barlovento/Gallegos road, follow it to the right. At the junction, turn left, then take the first right turn, just before a *casa forestal* (forestry house). This brings you to the centre of **Barlovento** (**4h10min**). The BUS STOP is 100m/yds below the CENTRO DL SALUD

3 LAS LOMADAS • BARRANCO DEL AGUA • LOS TILOS • LOS SAUCES

See map opposite; see also photograph page 47

Distance/time: 10km/6.2mi; 3h35min

Grade: strenuous. There's a lot of scrambling over rocks and boulders in the bed of the *barranco,* and a climb of 350m/1100ft to the *mirador.* You must be sure-footed and have a head for heights. Don't attempt just after rain or in very windy weather: the paths are dangerous if wet, and there is the possibility of rockfall in the *barranco. Yellow and white PR waymarking beyond Los Tilos*

NB: In summer the Los Sauces town hall diverts water from the canals to create a waterfall five minutes from the entrance to the Barranco del Agua. When this cascade is 'switched on', it is not possible to take the detour at the 1h-point: you can only go as far as the falls, and *a charge is made.* The local government also plans to introduce a year-round charge to visit Los Tilos, the watercourses and the Casa del Monte.

Equipment: hiking boots, sunhat, sunglasses, suncream, anorak, rain-gear, picnic, water

How to get there: 🚍 from Santa Cruz to Las Lomadas (Línea 2); alight just before the bridge over the Barranco del Agua; journey time 45min. *Hint: You will not see the bridge from the bus in time to alight, so make it clear to the driver that you are walking to Los Tilos.*

To return: 🚍 same bus from Los Sauces

Short walks

1   Los Tilos — Mirador de las Barandas — Los Tilos (2km/1.25mi; 1h). Grade (ascent) and equipment as main walk. 🚗 car or taxi to/from Los Tilos (car park). Climb the steep path ascending the hillside from the car park (behind the Interpretation Centre, the 2h-point in the main walk). Take care when returning: the descent is slippery!

2   Los Tilos — Barranco del Agua — Los Tilos (1km/0.6mi; 30min return). Easy, but you need to be agile — there's lots of scrambling over and around rocks (wear stout shoes with a good grip). Don't attempt in wet or windy weather. 🚗 as Short walk 1. From the car park walk down the asphalt road a short way, to locate a watercourse with adjacent path — on your right, just before the bridge. Pick up the main walk at the 1h-point and follow it to the first rock face (but see 'NB' above).

There's no *barranco* like this one in the whole archipelago. Its virtually perpendicular walls are smothered in vegetation, and from its boulder-strewn floor you look up at the sky through cascading ferns and trees. Only one thing is missing from the Barranco del Agua ... water. Narrow *canales* divert this precious commodity higher up the valley, transporting it to nearby villages and farms, and to a power plant that generates 10 per cent of the island's electricity. But although you can't see the water, you can *hear* it — in the *canales* above and beside you.

The walk begins in **Las Lomadas**, at the BUS STOP just south of the BRIDGE OVER THE BARRANCO DEL AGUA. Follow the road into the *barranco,* then take the left turn (**15min**) and ascend the road towards Los Tilos. After you cross the Barranco del Agua for the third time (**1h**), look below the road on the left for a watercourse with an adjacent path. *(Short Walk 2 joins here and turns right on the watercourse.)* Here we begin an hour-long foray into the dramatic innards of the *barranco*. Follow the path for a minute, until you reach a tank and a gate, then take steps down into the bed of the *barranco* and head upstream, scrambling over tree trunks, rocks and, eventually, boulders. After 15 minutes, the way is blocked by a 3m/10ft-high rock face. A path on the right-hand wall of the ravine circumvents it and drops you back into the *barranco* bed. *(This path is **dangerous**, but most people scramble up it nonetheless.)* The other alternative, just as dangerous, is to haul yourself up over a series of fallen trees. A little over 10 minutes further up the *barranco,* another sheer rock face is encountered — this one insurmountable.

Return down the *barranco* and back up to the road. Turn left to the car park and restaurant at **Los Tilos** and, above these, the INTERPRETATION CENTRE for the 'Los Tilos Biosphere Reserve' (**2h**). There is a large picnic area below the centre but, for a more peaceful picnic, try the setting shown below (Picnic 3): locate the watercourse two minutes' walk below the centre, and follow it to the left for a few minutes. The path is vertiginous, but a handrail *(don't lean on it)* provides psychological support.

The next part of the walk is the tiring climb to the Mirador de las Barandas. Take the yellow/white waymarked path behind the centre (large board: CAMINO AL MIRADOR DE LAS BARANDAS). There are no turn-offs. Handrails along the vertiginous stretches help allay any fears, but *don't lean on them!* Thirty-five minutes up, and blue in the face, you reach the **Mirador de las Barandas** (**2h35min**; photograph page 47), with a shelter, tables and benches, and a water tap. From here you look straight up the ravine as it twists and winds its way into the laurel woods of the central massif. Los Tilos lies below, in the narrow V of the *barranco*.

To make for Los Sauces, follow the track from the *mirador* to the main track and descend right on the PR LP7, ignoring all turn-offs. Through the trees and scrub you catch glimpses of the Barranco de Herradura (Walk 2), which soon drops away to your left. Some 30 minutes from the *mirador,* turn right on a cobbled path, just above an S-bend. After this short-cut you rejoin the main track on the very edge of the Barranco del Agua (**3h10min**) — with a bird's-eye view of your starting point.

Two minutes later the way becomes concreted and divides. Take the right fork, to begin the steep descent to Los Sauces. This pretty farming settlement is spread across a shoulder in the hillside, completely enveloped by banana plantations. Passing the *campo de fútbol*, you rejoin the left fork and continue downhill. A road joins from the right; a couple of minutes later, bear right at a fork. Multicoloured houses briefly flank the street leading into the centre of **Los Sauces** (**3h35min**). The BUS STOP is to the left of the main square, opposite the CHURCH.

Left: watercourse at Los Tilos (Picnic 3); right: in the Barranco del Agua the walls, dripping with vegetation, tower overhead and block out the sun.

4 LAS LOMADAS • LOS TILOS • NACIENTES DE CORDERO • NACIENTES DE MARCOS • LAS LOMADAS

Distance/time: 19km/12mi; 7h35min

Grade: very strenuous, with a drawn-out ascent of 1200m/3935ft and a descent of 1100m/3600ft. You must be sure-footed and have a head for heights: for over an hour the walk follows a *canal* cut into the sheer *barranco* wall. Only attempt this walk during a spell of fine, stable weather, and turn back *immediately* if the weather deteriorates. Do *not* attempt the walk immediately after bad weather, as there is a danger of rockfall and landslides. There are 13 tunnels on this walk, some narrow: not recommended for those who suffer from claustrophobia! *Yellow and white PR waymarks on most of the route*

NB: The local government plans to introduce a charge to visit Los Tilos, the watercourses and the Casa del Monte (price not known at press date).

Equipment: walking boots, raingear, jacket, trousers, picnic, water, *plus torch, large plastic bag, and an extra pair of socks* (one of the tunnels is as wet as a power shower: cover both yourself and your rucksack!).

How to get there: 🚌 from Santa Cruz to Las Lomadas (Línea 2); alight just before the bridge over the Barranco del Agua; journey time 45min
To return: 🚌 same bus from Las Lomadas to Santa Cruz

Short walk: Los Tilos — Mirador Espigón Atravesado — Los Tilos (5km/3mi; 1h30min). Moderate, with an ascent of 250m/820ft. Equipment as above (excluding tunnel equipment), but stout shoes will suffice. Access by 🚗: park at the foot of the first track on the left, 2km up the Los Tilos road (500m short of Los Tilos). (If you come by bus, allow an extra 55min each way from the bus stop by the bridge to the track where the walk begins and back down to the main road.) Follow the main walk from the 55min-point to the fork at the 1h45min-point. Just below it, take the path to the left, to a precarious and vertiginous viewpoint over the ravine (3-5min). Return the same way.

Alternative walk: Los Tilos — Nacientes de Cordero — Los Tilos (12.5km/8mi; 5h). Grade as main walk, excluding the *canal* stretch (sections of the route are vertiginous, but not for such prolonged periods). Access/return as for the *Short walk*. Follow the main walk to the 4h-point and return the same way.

This walk can be summed up in three words: exhilarating, breathtaking (in more ways than one), and tiring. You set off in a 'jungle' of laurel woods and huff and puff your way up to sheer-sided isolated valleys, not unlike those in the Caldera de Taburiente. Your reward is water splashing down out of the hillsides — the *nacientes* (springs) of Cordero and Marcos. Then you leave these isolated valleys via a *canal* with 13 tunnels — a marvel of workmanship. It's my favourite walk on the island, even though cliff-hanging *canales* give me the jitters.

The walk starts in **Las Lomadas**, at the BUS STOP just south of the BRIDGE OVER THE BARRANCO DEL AGUA. Follow the road into the *barranco,* then take the left turn (**15min**) and ascend the road towards Los Tilos. As you approach **Los Tilos**, look for a track on the left, next to a parking area, with a large sign, 'MONTE EL CANAL Y LOS TILOS' (**55min**). (This is some 500m short of the starting point for Walk 3, and there is also a large, confusing sign in three languages *and* a smaller signpost: NACIENTES DE MARCOS Y CORDERO, PR LP6, CAMINO DE LA RESERVA DE LA BIOSFERA.) The track is closed to motor traffic, but motorists doing the Short or Alternative walk can park off the road just beyond this track. Ascend the track, climbing steadily up the left side of the valley, at one point going through a 100m/yd-long tunnel. The *barranco* walls rise high above, and the stream bed lies far below. The way is cool and shaded with dense foliage.

Some 50 minutes up the track (**1h45min**), you come to a clearing with a sign. Your ongoing route is to the *right* but, just *before* the clearing, turn sharp left up a narrow, exposed path protected by wobbly guard rails. It climbs a thin blade of rock to the **Mirador Espigón Atravesado**, from where you will have an exhilarating view over the section of *barranco* already climbed.

Return to the track and continue uphill. *(But for the Short walk, return to Los Tilos.)* Some superb colonies of *Woodwardia radicans* (ferns) cascade out of the rocky barranco wall along this track. Less than 15 minutes above the *mirador* turn-off, a large sign 'SENDERO DE MARCOS Y CORDEROS — DANGEROUS WAY', calls you to a halt. *Please **read** this sign:* it's a warning about your ongoing route. But the sign predates the upgrading of this path; it is now a good walking trail, albeit vertiginous in places. The later section, along the *canal,* is potentially more hazardous.

Descend the steep narrow path behind the sign. A high rattly bridge takes you over the **Barranco Rivero**. Don't lean on the handrails! Over the bridge, turn left, uphill. The sheer hillsides are covered in dense vegetation. Coming out of the blanket of trees, a dramatic change in scenery takes place and the valley opens up ahead. The laurel wood vanishes and the walls become rocky, with pines clinging to the precipitous inclines. Almost before you realise it, the path has entered a side-*barranco* on the right (**2h45min**), where there is no vegetation to mask the sheer drops down to the left; there's risk of vertigo here.

Twenty minutes later you come to a fine VIEWPOINT over this alpine-like valley (**3h 05min**). Ignore the path off left a few minutes later. The valley closes up into a narrow passageway, and you round a corner to another rattly FOOTBRIDGE (**3h 15min**). Just over the bridge, follow the stream bed (SIGNPOST). This will take you up to the very foot of the first springs — the Nacientes de Cordero.

The *barranco* bed is bouldery and requires scrambling, occasionally on all fours. Little light penetrates this dark fissure. After 15 minutes in the *barranco*, take the path on the right (SIGNPOST). Continue straight on up through the next intersection, and minutes later cross the *barranco*. Then climb the hillside opposite, taking care on the narrow path covered in slippery pine needles. After a short stiff climb of a little over five minutes, you're back in the *barranco*, at a point where you are completely surrounded by high walls. The sound of gushing water heralds the still-hidden springs, which splash down out of the rock face above. Take any of the paths ascending to the right out of the *barranco* bed. Then turn left (where a signpost point right for Pico de la Cruz), cross the *barranco* at a large rockfall and ascend to the **Nacientes de Cordero** (**4h**). Having dragged

Right: some of the plants you will see on La Palma include (from top to bottom) taginaste, vinagrera, codeso, verode, red-flowering tabaiba and candelabra spurge.

You will follow this watercourse from the Nacientes de Marcos for well over an hour — until you reach the forestry track to the Casa del Monte. Sometimes you'll be walking on the very lip of the canal, but usually there is an adjacent path, as seen in this photograph.

yourself up to the foot of these mighty cliffs, no doubt you'll experience a great urge to stand right under one of the pounding cascades. (*The Alternative walk turns back here.*)

To move on to the Nacientes de Marcos, follow the *canal* fed by these springs. After five minutes you enter the first of the tunnels on the watercourse. Emerging from the tunnel three minutes later, you step out into a spectacular scene of vertical rock walls, very different from the Barranco Ribero in the earlier part of the hike. A couple of minutes further along, beckoned by the roar of water, leave the *canal* briefly — to descend steeply to the Nacientes de Marcos along a path with steps and protective wooden handrails.

Soon you're at the **Nacientes de Marcos (4h20min)**, and water is crashing down all around you. So much water, so much noise — it's terrifically exhilarating! Your aquatic adventure has now begun, so put on your plastic cover-up before going through the next tunnel. The *canal* path is your route for the next hour and 10 minutes. At times you will need to scramble up onto the edge of the *canal* itself but, in general, the path runs alongside it.

Some of the tunnels are quite a squeeze, very romantic ... especially when you meet a group of 20 other sweaty hikers halfway through! ***Very important:*** *Although the most dangerous parts of the path have been secured with wooden handrails, there are still many steep and narrow sections. Please watch where you're walking* **all the time***. To appreciate the magnificent scenery, stop walking, then look!*

Eventually the *canal* path moves back into the laurel wood and meets a forestry track, just above a forestry house. For the home stretch, walk 50m/yds down the track, then turn right on a path opposite the forestry house (**Casa del Monte**; **5h35min**). Three minutes down the path, where it veers to the right, take a narrow path at the left of this wide path, and follow it downhill. For the next 30 minutes your route goes straight down this dark, heavily-wooded path. Ignore all paths and tracks to the left or right, until you reach the MOTORABLE TRACK TO LAS LOMADAS (**6h05min**; SIGNPOST). Don't join the motor track here, but continue on the path; 20m further down you rejoin the track (SIGNPOST). Walk 15m/yds to the left and then branch off on the path again. When you next meet the track, follow it 50m/yds down to the left to rejoin the path (SIGNPOST). Next you emerge on a minor farm track: go 20m/yds to the right here, to pick up the path again, a deep trench cut into the hillside. A T-junction follows: turn right along the track. After one minute another track joins from the right. One minute later, at a three-way junction, cross a track and descend a COBBLED PATH (**6h40min**).

After five minutes the path meets the end of a track; turn left here. After another five minutes follow a concrete lane descending ahead. Two minutes later turn right along a track and, after 20m/yds, pick up the old path again. For the next five minutes keep straight downhill on this narrow path. Meet a track and follow it to the left. Cross another track and after 35m/yds, you can pick up the path, on the left. When you rejoin the MAIN TRACK at a fork, go left (SIGNPOST). At the junction that follows 30m/yds futher on, take the left fork (signpost, 'LAS LOMADAS'). At another junction three minutes downhill, turn right. Los Sauces sits on the slopes opposite. From here, just keep straight downhill, first on a track, then a concrete lane, and finally an asphalt road. Passing through **Las Lomadas**, you reach the LP1. The BUS STOP is just where you join the main road (**7h35min**).

5 BARRANCO DE LA GAL

Distance/time: 4.5km/3mi; 1h35min

Grade: easy, with a gradual ascent of 2
Recommended for everyone. *Yellow*
much of the way

Equipment: walking shoes, raingear,

How to get there and return: 🚌 fro
2); alight at the second tunnel just aft
stop); journey time about 30min; sam
the entrance to the track, just before th

Alternative walk: Barranco de la Galga — Cubo de la Galga — La Galga (6.75km/4.2mi; 1h40min). Grade as main walk. However, the path out of the *barranco* is vertiginous and potentially dangerous; you must be sure-footed and have a head for heights. Walking boots are recommended. Access as main walk, then take the same bus back from La Galga. Travelling by car, park in La Galga, and walk down to the Barranco de la Galga where the walk begins (adding 20min to the walking times). Follow the main walk to just past the 40min-point, to the recess in the valley wall. Facing the cliffs, take the path straight ahead that passes underneath the water *canal* through a little arch. Then, at the junction, turn left and follow this path along the steep *barranco*. Be careful after rainfall, parts of the path may have fallen away, making it considerably narrower. Within 20min, when you reach a concrete track (signpost: PR LP5.1, LA GALGA, SAN BARTOLOME), follow it downhill for one minute, when asphalt comes underfoot. A few minutes later, in a big bend to the right (with a SIGNPOST as above), turn left on a slippery cobbled path beside a pipe and follow it downhill. Descending first through a chestnut grove, then gardens, you reach a concrete lane. Follow the lane down past a line of houses. After 5min, cross straight over a road, onto a path. This takes you up an embankment and onto a driveway. You cross the road again, keeping straight down on a concrete lane which takes you under the road. Then cross the road once again and descend to the main road in La Galga (1h40min; signpost pointing in the opposite direction: CUBO DE LA GALGA, MIRADOR DE LA SOMADA ALTA). The bus stop is 5m/yds to the left of this junction.

Canary pine

Canary palm

Dragon tree

This walk is ideal for 'first timers'. It's just straight up and straight back without any paths turning off to confuse you, and you get a taste of La Palma's laurel forest without having to venture too far.

Begin at the BUS STOP AT THE TUNNEL: take the narrow road leading up the **Barranco de la Galga**. Ignore the track descending to the left. From the outset you can see that this is a deep ravine, with walls matted in vegetation. Billowing bushes of blackberry border the route. You pass a small grove of chestnut trees almost lost in this turmoil of vegetation. The sound of water trickling down the walls provides company for most of the way.

After **15min** the tarmac ends; the track passes below an AQUEDUCT (**25min**) and soon the floor of the *barranco* fills with laurel trees. Fifteen minutes later both the *barranco* and the track fork (**40min**). First try the left fork.

This track ends almost immediately, but a path leads up to a small waterfall (in winter) in a few minutes. *Geranium canariense* abounds along the floor of the *barranco*. On the left lies a beautiful recess in the valley wall, shaded by tall thin trees, where you will see a *canal* and a large water pipe. *(Those doing the Alternative walk turn left just past the* canal, *but first have a look into the right fork of the* barranco.)

Return and walk up the right fork, then turn right on an overgrown track. This quickly peters out into a path and ends at a rock cauldron, the **Cubo de la Galga** (**55min**). Quarrying once took place here, but now the massive escarpment has reverted to nature. After heavy rain a pretty waterfall flows down the hanging valley opposite.

Allow yourself about 40min to return to the BUS STOP ON THE MAIN ROAD (**1h35min**). If you've plenty of time to spare before the bus, there's a bar-restaurant in La Galga, 20 minutes uphill to the right, and another bus stop just beyond it (where a lane ascends to the right).

Laurel forest in the Barranco de la Galga

6 LP4 (PICO DE LA NIEVE TURN-OFF) • PICO DE LA NIEVE • PUNTA DE LOS ROQUES • ERMITA DE LA VIRGEN DEL PINO • NATIONAL PARK VISITOR CENTRE

Distance/time: 16km/10mi; 5h45min

Grade: moderate but long, with an initial ascent of 300m/1000ft and a descent of 1400m/4600ft. Accessible to all sturdy hill walkers who are sure-footed and have a head for heights, but only suitable in fine weather. Avoid on very windy days. At certain times of the year the path may be overgrown with *codeso*. **Important:** *weather conditions can change rapidly; be prepared! If cloud descends,* **utmost care** *is needed, as the walk passes along the rim of the crater for much of the way. Both yellow and white (PR) and red and white (GR) waymarking*

Equipment: walking boots, sunhat (and something to tie it on with!), sunglasses, suncream, long-sleeved shirt, long trousers, warm cardigan, warm jacket, gloves, raingear, picnic, plenty of water

How to get there: 🚖 taxi to the Pico de la Nieve turn-off on the LP4; journey time 50min from Santa Cruz
To return: 🚌 from the National Park Visitor Centre (Línea 1) — to Santa Cruz (journey time 40min) or Los Llanos (journey time 20min)

Short walk: LP4 (Pico de la Nieve turn-off) to Pico de la Nieve and return (4.75km/3mi; 2h). Moderate ascent of 300m/1000ft. Equipment and access as main walk or 🚖 car to parking area at the end of the Pico de la Nieve track (deduct 100m/330ft; 20min of climbing at the outset). Follow the main walk to the 1h15min-point, then turn left. Ten minutes later rejoin your outgoing path and turn right downhill, back to your car.

Alternative walks

1 Cruce del Refugio — Ermita de la Virgen del Pino — Reventón Pass — Refugio El Pilar — National Park Visitor Centre (16.5km/10mi; 5h20min). Strenuous, with an ascent of 580m/1900ft. Equipment as main walk. Access by 🚌 to Cruce del Refugio (Línea 1); journey time from Santa Cruz 40min. From the junction where you leave the bus walk north along the main road for 50m/yds, then turn left on a country road. Use the map to walk to the Ermita de la Virgen del Pino (40min) and then ascend to the Reventón Pass (1h55min). Turn right at the pass and, referring to the map on pages 68-69, follow the track to the Refugio El Pilar (3h35min). To end the walk, pick up Walk 7 at the 2h20min-point.

2 Ermita de la Virgen del Pino — Refugio de la Punta de los Roques — Ermita de la Virgen del Pino (17km/10.5mi; 6h10min). Very strenuous, with an ascent of 1250m/4100ft. Only suitable in fine weather. Equipment as main walk. Access by 🚖: park at the *ermita,* north of the National Park Visitor Centre. Or 🚌 to/from the National Park Visitor Centre (Línea 1; journey time from Santa Cruz 40min; add 30min *each way* to the walking times above). Referring to the map on page 63, follow this section of the main walk in reverse — from either the *ermita* or the visitor centre; return the same way.

I consider this one of the top walks in the Canaries. Circling the Caldera de Taburiente, often on its very rim, spectacular views stretch away before you. On the descent your outlook sweeps across the plain of Los Llanos, over the volcanoes of El Pilar, and along the *cumbre*. If you're reasonably fit, this is one walk you've got to do! And the good news is that a taxi or your hired car will do most of the climbing for you.

Start out at the PICO DE LA NIEVE TURN-OFF. Walk up the LP4 for 6m/yds, then take the hillside path above the road (signpost: PICO LA NIEVE, PR LP3). After a couple of minutes, the path swings back to the left, then climbs a gentle slope and widens out. Cairns mark the way through a typical Canary pine forest — spacious and with a floor clear of scrub. The path takes you to a CAR PARK (*where the Short walk can begin and end;* **20min**) and continues uphill for another 15 minutes; here you turn right on the path to the summit (SIGNPOST). Your view stretches across the forested shoulders of the *cumbre*. On clear days Tenerife and La Gomera are clearly visible in the distance. Santa Cruz sits far below.

Approaching the edge of the crater, turn right uphill on the GR131, the RUTA DE LA CRESTERIA (signpost: ROQUE DE LOS MUCHACHOS). (Ignore signposting for the Refugio del Pilar to the left.) At the next fork, keep left (the right-hand fork leads to Roque de los Muchachos). From the SUMMIT OF **Pico de la Nieve** (**1h**) a breathtaking view opens before you, of a deep cauldron lined by sheer tumbling ridges. The white buildings peeping over the crater walls on the right belong to the observatory shown on page 18.

Return to the Roque de los Muchachos junction and turn right; turn right again at the next fork (signpost: REFUGIO DEL PILAR). A path joins from the left (**1h15min**); follow it to the right. (*But for the Short walk, turn left here.*) After a few minutes, you cross the pass (**Degollada del Barranco de la Madera**; signposted). Here you'll notice some very colourful rocky outcrops rising out of the crater wall. A few minutes later you encounter a signposted turn-off to some petroglyphs ('PETROGLIFO TAGOROR PICO DE LA SABINA'). Shortly, pass a bald gravel mound in hues of mauve, pink, smokey blue, and rusty brown.

The next section of the hike is the most striking. A zig-zag descent leads you down and across another pass— the **Degollada del Río** (**2h05min**). The ridge here is very narrow and slides away on either side of the path. The huge valley to the left is the Barranco de la Hortelana, while to the right the crater just opens into a bottomless abyss. A steep climb follows, up the side of a precipitous jagged crag. Back on the inside of the crater, you pass by the eye-catching weather-beaten *cedro* shown overleaf. Ahead is a magnificent viewpoint. In the depths of this cataclysm of rock, you can see the floor of the Barranco

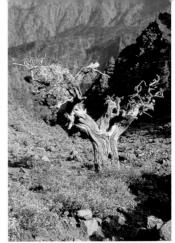

Right: a noticeable weather-beaten cedro is passed just before the refuge; far right: striding along the cumbre on the descent to Reventón Pass. Below left: leaving the Cruce del Refugio, you soon look across a basin of fields criss-crossed by stone walls (Alternative walk 1). Below right: view south from the Refugio de la Punta de los Roques over the El Paso basin to the Cumbre Vieja

de Taburiente and a corner of the Playa de Taburiente (Walk 11). Then you round a bend and arrive at the **Refugio de la Punta de los Roques (2h35min)**. Although there is no heating, bedding or fireplaces, the shelter may be welcome nonetheless. The slope falling from the refuge overlooks the extensive open valleys of El Paso and Los Llanos and, in the background, Cumbre Vieja (Walk 9).

Continuing, pick up the path below the refuge. The route descends the *cumbre,* never straying far from the crest, and passes below the summits of **Pico Corralejo** and then **Pico Ovejas**. Ignore two paths to the left (5min and 15min past the sign for Pico Ovejas). The western side of the *cumbre* opens up, affording another fine view over Santa Cruz. The path finally drops down onto the **Pista Cumbre Nueva**. Continue ahead on this wide forestry track. Some 20 minutes later you arrive at **Reventón**

Pass (**4h25min**), where there is a WATER TAP. Fork right downhill here on the PR LP1 (signpost: ERMITA DE LA VIRGEN DEL PINO).

A beautiful old cobbled path leads you down the steep slope, below trees festooned with lichen and beside moss-covered rocks. A basin of small fenced-off fields lies below. Five minutes down, a path joins from the right. Some 35 minutes down, the path meets a minor track, which leads you down through a splendid avenue of regal Canary pines, some of them reputed to be 400 to 500 years old. Finally you arrive at the **Ermita de la Virgen del Pino** (**5h15min**; Picnic 6).

The National Park Visitor Centre is just under half an hour away: follow the road away from the chapel and, after 15 minutes, at a junction, turn left. On reaching the LP3, turn left again to the **Visitor Centre** (**5h45min**). The Santa Cruz bus stops opposite.

7 LOMO DE LOS MESTRES • LA PARED VIEJA • REFUGIO EL PILAR • NATIONAL PARK VISITOR CENTRE

Distance/time: 14km/8mi; 4h

Grade: moderate; gradual ascent of 450m/1500ft. Not recommended in wet weather. *Yellow and white PR waymarking for most of the way. Note: new paths and tracks are established in this area every few months, to reach wood-cutting areas and newly-established fields. Some new paths and tracks may be missing from the text and the maps, but the walk is easily followed if you watch for the signposts and waymarks. Around the Pared Vieja picnic area, do* not *follow the small white/green signposts, but the white/yellow waymarking.*

Equipment: walking shoes, sunhat, sunglasses, suncream, raingear, warm cardigan, anorak, picnic, water

How to get there: 🚌 Los Llanos bus *from Santa Cruz* (Línea 1). ***Important notes:*** There are two tunnels on the LP3 below Cumbre Nueva, and traffic is one-way: from Santa Cruz to Los Llanos through the old tunnel and from Los Llanos to Santa Cruz through the newer, lower tunnel. The walk is only accessible from the *older tunnel*. If you are taking a bus from Los Llanos, you must go into Santa Cruz and then switch to a bus travelling *back* to Los Llanos. (If you are travelling by taxi from Los Llanos, your driver will have to go through the new tunnel first, then head back up the *cumbre* towards the old tunnel.) By bus or taxi, ask to be dropped off just before the 'túnel viejo', an *unofficial bus stop* not far below the old tunnel; journey time 35min from Santa Cruz. ***Important note:*** despite the fact that there is a large lay-by before the tunnel and this walk is in all the guides, some drivers *refuse to stop*. Before you board, ask for '**el túnel viejo de la cumbre para la pista de los lomos a Pared Vieja**'; if necessary, show the driver this text or the map. Do not board unless you have the driver's agreement, because you cannot alight past the tunnel and walk back (walking and cycling through the tunnel is forbidden). If the driver refuses, you will have to take a taxi. *To return:* 🚌 same bus from the National Park Visitor Centre; journey time 40min to Santa Cruz

Short walks

1   Refugio El Pilar — Lomo de los Mestres (8.75km/5.4mi; 2h25min). Easy descent of 450m/1500ft. Equipment as main walk. Access by 🚗 taxi or with friends to the Refugio El Pilar. Use the map to do the main walk in reverse. Return by bus to *Los Llanos* (Línea 1) from the tunnel entrance where the track ends on the LP3. There is *no* official bus stop here, so head down the road to where you can *flag down* the bus.

2   Refugio El Pilar — National Park Visitor Centre (6.5km/4mi; 2h). Easy, with a descent of 600m/1950ft. Equipment as main walk. Access as *Short walk 1*. Follow the main walk from just after the 2h20min-point to the end and return as in the main walk.

Alternative walk: Lomo de los Mestres — La Pared Vieja — Cumbre Nueva — Mazo (16.5km/10.3mi; 4h50min). Moderate, with an ascent of 450m/1500ft and a descent of 950m/3100ft, much of it down an old cobbled path (slippery in wet weather). Equipment and access as main walk. Return by bus to Santa Cruz (Línea 3) or pick up a taxi when you reach Mazo. I highly recommend this hike: the stretch from the Pista Cumbre Nueva to Mazo follows one of the finest old *caminos* (cobbled trails) on the island. Follow the main walk up to the 2h20min-point, where it briefly joins the Pista Cumbre Nueva. From here follow the El Pilar/San Isidro road uphill to the left. After 400m/yds, note a forestry track to the right called Pista Llano la Mosca. Some 55m/yds beyond this track, turn left between two low stone walls (yellow and white waymarking). Soon you cross a wooden bridge and then continue on a minor track. A couple of minutes along, turn right on a path (signpost: 'MAZO, CAMINO DE LA FAYA, PR LP17') and cross another wooden bridge. Cross the track again and, a few minutes later, cross the road to San Isidro by a wooden building (2h35min; signpost). Continue on the path that first veers sharply right and then left (by an enormous pine). After five minutes, join the Mazo track. Turn right and, after 20m/yds, turn left down a path (signpost). Cross another wooden bridge and rejoin the track. Turn left and, after 50m/yds (ignoring a first turn-off to the left), turn left on the Camino de la Faya (signposted; 2h45min), immediately passing behind a shed and a house. Pass a viewpoint and, one minute later (some 25m/yds after a minor track forks left), take the path going left (signpost). Ignore the faint path ascending to the right shortly after, as well as a signposted path on the right. Next, cross a minor track, only to rejoin it a minute later and follow it downhill. Another track now joins from the right. Almost immediately, at a T-junction, turn right (waymark). Another T-junction follows, where you turn right again. Two minutes later, ignore a track on the left (signpost). Within two minutes you descend to an intersection of four tracks, where you turn left (signpost). Ignore any faint turn-offs or tracks until, after five minutes, you pass an apple orchard and join a track (signpost). Follow the track to the right for 150m/yds, then turn onto the path again. The path crosses several tracks in the next 15 minutes (sometimes joining the track for 10 or 20m/yds; each junction is signposted or waymarked). When the path eventually widens into a track, turn right down to the road to the Mazo dump (signpost; 3h40min). Turn left here and, when you reach the gates to the dump, descend to the right on a path. At the next track crossing, turn left (signpost) to pick up the continuing path. Twenty minutes later, cross a track and then a covered *canal*. Just below the *canal* you join a track and follow it downhill, crossing another track a minute later. The way finally joins a concrete lane, which you descend. On reaching a maze of country lanes, bear left after the third lane and descend a paved lane (signpost: PLAYA DEL HOYO, PR LP17). The tarmac ends shortly; continue straight downhill. Cross a minor track and continue on the steep concreted track to the left of a water tank. After a few minutes you arrive on the Mazo road in La Rosa (4h35min), just

The Llano del Jable, a plain of pitch-black sand (Picnic 7c)

ifteen minutes along to the right. Keep right
e road: the bus stop is just past the fork, and
along (4h50min).

roduction to La Palma. Your views
e eastern and western slopes of the
untainous spine. And how different
orth is verdant with woodlands, the
nic splendour with a desert of black

taña Quemada

Alight from the bus at the large lay-by east of the old tunnel on the LP3, at a place called **Lomo de los Mestres**. To **begin the walk**, head south on the forestry track by the tunnel entrance. Straight away you're engulfed by a dense mantle of trees and bushes. This evergreen forest, mainly composed of four types of laurel, covered much of southern Europe and North Africa some 15-40 million years ago. Unfortunately, little remains of this unique woodland, the Canary Islands and Madeira being its last refuge.

You snatch glimpses of San Pedro and some adjacent villages over the verdant slopes of the island's high eastern midriff. The only sounds will be birdsong and lizards torpedoing up the banks. After a gradual ascent you reach **La Pared Vieja**, a picnic area (**1h45min**; Picnic 7a). Apart from weekends, when it is very busy, this cool, shady *zona recreativa* makes a good resting place. Follow the track straight on through the picnic area until you meet the El Pilar/San Isidro road (LP301). Don't follow it; instead, turn up to the right by a large information board and a sign, 'PARQUE NATURAL', and follow an old cobbled trail with yellow and white PR waymarks that passes above and to the left of the picnic area. Ignore small side paths and a track coming in from the left. In two minutes you join a track coming from the right. When the track swings right two minutes later, keep straight ahead along a path. Cross the track and again rejoin the old path, as it ascends to the left. You pass a shrine on the right immediately. The *camino* climbs steadily, threading its way through the canopy of trees and shrubs.

Some 25 minutes up from the road, the path leaves the canopy of trees and widens out. At a small junction, turn left uphill on another path (signpost: REFUGIO DEL PILAR, PR LP18). Volcanic mounds begin appearing through the trees. A shallow V in the ridge leads you up to an earthen road — the **Pista Cumbre Nueva (2h20min**; SIGNPOST). Turn left along this road. *(Short walk 2 begins here, and Alternative walk 6-1 joins here.)* Then turn right down the El Pilar road, past the **Refugio El Pilar** picnic area (Picnic 7b). *(But for the Alternative walk, turn left up this road, towards San Isidro.)*

Some 100m/yds from the entrance to the *refugio* (which has a modest visitors' centre), turn right (sign on a tree, 'ACAMPADA', indicating a camping ground). Keep to the left of the showers and a shallow gully; after 50m/yds you will come upon a beautiful old waymarked path between the pines. After 15 minutes you come out of the trees into a stunning volcanic landscape, with magnificent views of the *caldera.* Cross the road (signpost, 'PR LP14, EL PASO, TACONDE') and continue on the path, beginning your descent to **Montaña Quemada** — the prominent dark brown volcanic cone seen to your right.

When you meet the road again, don't follow it. Turn left onto the **Llano del Jable** and follow the main track for 200m/yds, then turn right on another track (signpost: 'EL PASO, PR LP14'). After another 200m/yds, at a junction of tracks, turn right (**2h50min**). A steep rough descent takes you into a scattering of pines. Ten minutes down this track (**3h**), ignore a track off left.

This is followed by another track descending from the left: without joining this second track, turn right on a wide path bordered by sagging stone walls (photograph page 70). A few minutes later cross the track. When you join the track again almost immediately, turn left. After a minute asphalt comes underfoot: turn right here, to rejoin the path. The way widens into a track. Fields of cultivated broom lie to the right. Keeping straight down, cross the road. After five minutes more, join the road again and follow it downhill. After ten minutes, at a junction of tracks all branching off to the left, descend the third track on the left (SIGNPOST; the initial few metres are paved).

When you rejoin the road (**3h40min**), turn left. The main road (LP3), a watering hole *(fuente),* and the bus shelter lie barely 10 minutes away (**3h50min**). There is another BUS STOP 10 minutes along to the right (**4h**) where, if you've time to spare, you can call in at the National Park Visitor Centre across the road.

8 LOS CANARIOS (FUENCALIENTE) • VOLCAN DE SAN ANTONIO • VOLCAN DE TENEGUIA • FARO DE FUENCALIENTE

See also photograph pages 22-23

Distance/time: 8km/5mi; 1h50min (16km/10mi; 4h20min if you return the same way)

Grade: moderate, with a descent of 700m/2300ft on gravel slopes (steep and stony in places). You must be sure-footed and have a head for heights, but this walk is *recommended for everyone* (there is only one very short stretch that might prove unnerving for those who suffer from vertigo). It is usually very windy here, especially around the volcanoes. Don't ascend to the rim of the Volcán de Teneguía in strong winds! *Note:* this is a very popular walk, and the restaurant at the Faro de Fuencaliente (lighthouse) is always full by mid-afternoon. *Red and white GR waymarking for most of the way*

Equipment: walking boots, sunhat, sunglasses, suncream, long trousers, cardigan, anorak, raingear, swimwear, picnic, plenty of water

How to get there: 🚌 from Los Llanos or Santa Cruz to Los Canarios (Línea 3); journey time 35-40min

To return: 🚗 Arrange in Los Canarios for a taxi to collect you from El Faro (the lighthouse), for your return bus (Línea 3).

Short walk: Volcán de San Antonio — Roque Teneguía — Volcán de Teneguía — Volcán de San Antonio (6km/3.5mi; 1h40min). Easy, but there is a stiff climb of 200m/650ft at the end. Equipment as above, but stout shoes will suffice. Access by 🚗: park at the Volcán de San Antonio (leave Los Canarios on the Las Indias road and, just past the last houses, turn left on a gravel track to the car park (fee payable). Follow the main walk from the 10min-point to the 1h05min-point, then retrace steps.

The Volcán de Teneguía is one of the most colourful volcanoes on La Palma, and the combination of striking coastal scenery and intriguing volcanic landscape make this a 'not to be missed' hike. Faro de Fuencaliente is today a working fishing hamlet, with an authentic restaurant, where the smiling *señora* serves up hearty fishermen's portions.

Begin the walk at the BAR PARADA in **Los Canarios** (it's 200m/yds west of the bus stop on the main road). Walk down the narrow street opposite the bar, descending past a telephone box. Go through a junction and reach the LAS INDIAS ROAD. Follow this to the right downhill and, after 100m/yds fork right on a road. (This fork is just beyond the turn-off for the Bodega Llanovid — also known as Bodega Teneguía and visited in Car tour 2.) You pass an *urbanización* on the right. Descending, you look straight onto the dark, flat-topped Volcán de San Antonio. Crossing the Las Indias road again (by a large, confusing sign and map), follow the gravel track that heads for the crater. On reaching the pay booth for the VISITORS' CENTRE, go straight ahead on the waymarked path at the right-hand side of the **Volcán de San Antonio** (**10min**). (*The Short* *walk starts here.*) A spectacular view opens up across hillside vineyards to Las Indias on your right; the sheer slopes of the western escarpment fill the backdrop, and you can see Puerto Naos, a handful of buildings backing onto a sea-flat of banana plantations. The crater rim is narrow in places, and some people may find a short stretch vertiginous. Roque Teneguía is the yellow rock jutting out of the hillside below. The southern coast unfolds, with El Faro sitting near the southernmost tip, by glaring-white salt pans. But it's the magically-coloured Volcán de Teneguía that holds your gaze. It used to be possible to circle the whole crater on this path, but today it has been closed off halfway round for conservation reasons, so you will have to retrace your steps.

Return to the VISITORS' CENTRE, and now descend a path below the car park (signpost: TENEGUIA, FARO DE FUEN-CALIENTE, GR131, RUTA DE LOS VOLCANES). A steep, gravelly and dusty descent brings you down to a track: turn left. Rounding the slopes, you look down on Roque Teneguía. Banana plantations and greenhouses vie to smother the coastal flat. Barely five minutes along the track, fork right on a clear path descending to **Roque Teneguía** (**45min**). This hunk of rock, although not large, is a prominent landmark and a good viewing point for the coastal banana plantations. While you are here, have a search for petro-glyphs; there are several of them on the sloping side of the rock, but they are quite faded.

To continue, take the stone-marked path opposite the rock for three minutes, until you reach the *canal.* Turn left along the *canal.* Shiny-leafed *vinagrera* (of the dock family) flourishes here. After a few minutes, descend to a track seen below and follow it to the left, towards the volcano. Then take a path off right, to the edge of the **Volcán de Teneguía** (**1h05min**).

(A path ascends the left-hand rim of this spectacularly-coloured crater. It's a stupendous climb, *but very dangerous in a strong wind.* If it's calm and you make this ascent, add 20 minutes to the total time for the walk. Inside the crater, holes in the left-hand wall emit hot gases.)

The main walk continues by retracing

Top: smooth rolling slopes on the descent to the lighthouse.
Middle: Roque Teneguía.
Bottom: the Volcán de San Antonio, with Los Canarios in the background

Above: descending to the lighthouse; left: at the beach

the path for barely a minute, to a bend. Here descend a waymarked path to the right, down into the lava. Keep between Teneguía and its offspring (a baby volcano) on the left. A clear path soon leads you to a track, where you turn right. Within minutes, at a junction, turn right again on a cleared path through an intriguing lava stream. The twisted and jagged rock here is spellbinding.

Out of the lava stream, your path crosses smooth rolling slopes. As you mount a crest, the pink-tinted salt pans and the lighthouse appear not far below. On arriving at the ROAD TO THE LIGHTHOUSE (**1h30min**; SIGNPOST), turn right for 50m/yds, then pick up the continuation of your path on the left (SIGNPOST). Five minutes later cross the road once more (SIGNPOST). Passing close to the edge of the cliffs, you have a good view over Playa Nueva, embraced by a lava flow.

Cross the road yet again and descend towards the tiny fishing hamlet of **Faro de Fuentcaliente** (**1h50min**). It's a desolate yet striking spot. Parched, windswept and covered in dust, you're just in the mood for a dip … and then it's lunchtime. There's a small but interesting marine visitors' centre in the lighthouse. The restaurant is open from 13.00-18.00; closed Wednesdays. *Buen provecho!*

If you're returning on foot, allow 2h45min: follow the GR131, *avoiding* the steep short-cut at the right of Volcán de San Antonio, which is suffering badly from erosion from walkers try to find firm grip in the loose volcanic ash.

9 RUTA DE LOS VOLCANES

Map begins below and ends on page 80

Distance/time: 18km/11.25mi; 6h10min

Grade: fairly strenuous: although the ascent is only 500m/1600ft, the walk is very long, and much of it crosses volcanic gravel. Recommended only in fine weather: when the Cumbre Vieja is under cloud or mist, it's very easy to stray off the path, and *this could be dangerous.* Can be cold and windy. One short stretch demands a head for heights. *Red and white GR waymarking; some green and white SL waymarking*

Equipment: walking boots, sunhat, sunglasses, suncream, raingear, warm cardigan, anorak, picnic, plenty of water

How to get there: 🚖 taxi or with friends to the Refugio El Pilar
To return: 🚌 from Los Canarios to Santa Cruz or Los Llanos (Línea 3); journey time 35-40min

Shorter walk: El Pilar — Volcán Deseada — El Pilar (13km/8.1mi; 3h50min). Grade, equipment and access as main walk. Follow the main walk to the 2h15min-point and return the same way.

Here's a walk to rival Tenerife's Cañadas or Lanzarote's Timanfaya. You go from one volcano to another, and each is more impressive than the last. Magnificent views lure you on, surround you, and trail behind you. By the time you reach Los Canarios, you'll have seen enough volcanoes to last a lifetime.

The walk starts by the PUBLIC TOILETS in the **Refugio El Pilar** picnic area (Picnic 7b). Some 50m/yds beyond

Setting off from the Refugio El Pilar early in the morning, overlooking the Llano del Jable (Picnics 7b-c).

(south of) this building, turn right on a path opposite a WATER TANK (signpost: LOS CANARIOS, GR131, RUTA DE LOS VOLCANES). A steep ascent up through a pine wood follows. Under 10 minutes uphill, at a fork, keep right. Soon you're following a well-manicured path around the steep slopes of a volcano. A few minutes further up, a *mirador* provides an ideal spot to watch clouds swirling over the *cumbre*. Leaving the pines, a fine panorama unfolds: the hillsides slide down into the pine-studded basin cradling the Llano del Jable. Beyond these dark sands lie grassy fields, below the walls of the crater and the *cumbre*. El Paso spreads around the tail of a lava tongue, and Los Llanos is swallowed up amidst banana plantations.

Walk round the hillside (ignoring any paths that ascend to the left), and descend to a TRACK (**45min**; SIGNPOST). Turn left uphill and, after 15 minutes, turn right on a wide path (initially flanked by stone walls; SIGNPOST), into a 'rock garden' of *codeso (Adenocarpus)* and chrysanthemums.

Cross a WOODEN BRIDGE (**1h20min**) and, a good five minutes later, ignore two paths to the left (SIGNPOST). During the next 15 minutes you skirt a jagged-edged crater on the right. This is **Hoyo Negro** (the 'black hollow'; SIGNPOST), looking exactly like its name. Ten minutes later, you're peering down into a lava lake, the **Cráter del Duraznero** (**1h55min**). Descend to the right of this cone and, after eight minutes, at a fork, turn left uphill. (You will rejoin the right-hand fork further on.) Just below the edge of the brilliantly-coloured **Volcán Deseada** (**2h15min**), the path forks to encircle it. Take the right fork.

Left: climbing above the Refugio El Pilar at the start of the walk. Right: looking back along the route, not far beyond Volcán Deseada. Below: at 3h10min the best views on the hike unfold, when Volcán Martín is seen ahead.

A minute later the crater tumbles away below you. A twin crater, to the left of the main one, emanates equally striking pastel hues — orange, pink, yellow and cream. (*The Shorter walk returns from here.*)

Leaving Deseada, you mount a neck of ridge, and ascend to yet another crater (**2h35min**). Remain on the crest and then, just below the rim of the crater, turn right uphill. This crater offers a spectacular view along the volcanic spine of its dark naked slopes. Swifts by the score whistle past. Bearing round to the right, you pass a CONCRETE POST. Just below the post, you rejoin the path that forked right just beyond El Duraznero. Continue straight downhill here, by forking left. Leaving a shallow basin (SIGNPOST), you cross a low crest. At a crossroads of paths (SIGNPOST) carry straight on, and ignore a faint fork to the left. Entering a long shallow valley (**3h10min**), head across the sand and continue straight downhill (SIGNPOST); the odd survey post and stones intermittently line the path.

Soon (**3h45min**) the best views of the hike unfold. The sea appears just over the edge of the sandy volcanic slopes, with the reddish-pink cone of Volcán Martín stealing the show. Luminous green pines dot the immediate hillsides. Within 10 minutes, at a major fork on the slopes of **Volcán Martín** (**4h**; SIGNPOST), turn left. Turn left again at the fork that follows immediately. A minute downhill you're looking straight down into Volcán Martín, its rim ablaze with shades of mauve, cream and orange. Opposite, you can see a spring in a cave beside the crater floor. This is your last volcano, I promise.

Return to the forks and take the second left. (Or, if you're a glutton for punishment, take the first left, to ascend the crater rim and take in the extravaganza of volcanic hues shown above — as well as a good view

'Gluttons for punishment' can take a 15-minute detour along the rim of Volcán Martín to enjoy this extravaganza of volcanic hues.

over the southern tip of the island. Allow an extra 15 minutes for this.)

Continuing, just head straight downhill, ploughing down through the fine gravel — great fun. Just below Volcán Martín turn right at a fork, *leaving* the main GR131 path for another well-trodden path with green and white SL way-marking (signpost, 'Fuente del Tion').

When you come to a TRACK (**4h35min**), cross it (signpost: Los Canarios por Pista). Then descend for a few minutes, to a junction (SIGNPOST). Take the lower, left-hand track here and, from now on, just follow the signs for 'Los Canarios'. (After about 55 minutes the track crosses the original GR131 footpath to Los Canarios. If you decide to take this short-cut, turn right here. After three minutes cross another footpath and after another few minutes cross the track, to continue along the path, rejoining the main walk.)

Attention is needed around 1h down the main track (**5h40min**), when you are circling to the right of a vineyard set amidst crumbling stone walls. Here, ignore a minor turn-off left, after which a track joins you from the left. Ignore the signposted path to the right, and continue on the track towards Los Canarios. A few minutes later, keep an eye out for a WATER TANK on the right. Some 30m/yds past the tank, turn left on a path (signpost: 'GR131') and follow it straight downhill, picking up red and white waymarking again. On reaching the track again, follow it to the left (SIGNPOST). Soon you pass a basin of gardens set amidst pines. Some 50m/yds further on, take the path to the left (SIGNPOST). Los Canarios comes into sight just below, through the trees. Keep left at a fork. On meeting the track again, cross it and continue on the path (SIGNPOST). Emerging on a street in **Los Canarios** (**6h05min**), follow it 100m/yds downhill to the MAIN ROAD. Turn left and walk past Bar Parada (where Walk 8 begins). The BUS STOP is just three minutes further on; a bus shelter is opposite (**6h10min**).

10 PICO BEJENADO

See also photograph page 6   **Distance:** 12.5km/8mi; 4h25min

Grade: strenuous, with an ascent/descent of 700m/2300ft, but suitable for anyone who is reasonably fit. You must be sure-footed, and a few stretches demand a head for heights. Only suitable in fine weather; should clouds descend, the utmost care needed, especially at the summit. If a strong wind is blowing, keep away from rim of the crater. Signposting and yellow/white waymarking (PR LP13,3).

Equipment: walking boots, sunhat, sunglasses, suncream, raingear, long-sleeved shirt, long trousers, warm cardigan, warm jacket, gloves, picnic, plenty of water

How to get there and return: 🚗 car to/from El Barrial, above Valencia. Turn off the El Paso/Santa Cruz LP3 road for 'Parque Nacional' (at the visitor centre). Keep straight on at the first junction but, shortly after, turn left for Valencia. Keep ahead on this road and park when it reverts to very rough track. (There is another parking area further up this track, at the point where the ascent proper begins and the road is once again surfaced; you may prefer to park there if you are in a 4WD vehicle.)

Pico Bejenado, like Pico de la Nieve, is accessible to everyone, and for this reason alone, worth the effort of the ascent. You'll feel like an eagle once on the summit, as you peer down into every corner of the Caldera de Taburiente (Walk 11). And on the ascent you have a sweeping vista over the Los Llanos basin as it spills out into the sea. This hike offers a superlative of views.

These hike timings begin at the point where the asphalt *first* ends (signpost: 'PR LP13,3 BEJENADO'). Follow the track ahead to the turn-off point for the ascent of the peak, by a large park INFORMATION BOARD and a second parking

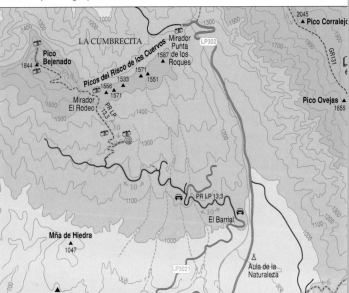

area with SIGNPOST (**20min**). Ignore a track to the right which comes up immediately. At a junction (**35min**) go left (signposted 'PICO BEJENADO'). Ignore a strong path ascending to the right just past the junction. The hillsides are wooded in Canary pines, and bare of undergrowth. Pico Bejenado is the peak furthest to the left in the wall of mountains ahead.

You come to another SIGNPOST (**1h**), pointing your way up a minor track to the right. Some minutes up, the track ends and a clear path takes over, zigzagging up the hillside. A little over five minutes later, keep left at a fork (sign: PETROGLIFOS 130M). But it's worth taking the short detour to right, to see the large petroglyph and take in the excellent views over the mountains near La Cumbrecita. The ascent steepens as you mount the shoulder of the crater, but the panorama expands to encompass the west coast, where a gentle built-up plain fans out from the basin of fields tucked back into the *cumbre*.

Soon (**1h45min**) the rim of the crater is just before you. You look down into a pine speckled *caldera*. More than likely the far walls of the crater will be under a mantle of clouds, which only enhances the picture. A minute further up, a sign tells you that this is the **Mirador El Rodeo**.

Forty minutes above the mirador, you finally reach the summit, **Pico Bejenado** (**2h25min**), with a bird's-eye view over the whole crater, lined by streams of ridges pouring down off the encircling wall of mountains. The strip of barranco bed visible below is the Playa de Taburiente. If you scramble down the 2m/6ft-high rock-face on the west side of the summit and continue to the end of the ridge, you will be able to look down into the Barranco de las Angustias and trace the forestry track up its far wall to Los Brecitos, where Walk 11 begins.

Return the same way, allowing 2h to regain the LOWER CAR PARK (**4h25min**).

On the rim of the crater, just above the Mirador El Rodeo

11 CALDERA DE TABURIENTE

See also photographs pages 9 and 26-27

Distance/time: 12.5km/7.8mi; 5h

Grade: long and quite strenuous, with a descent of 1000m/3300ft, but accessible to all fit walkers who are sure-footed and have a head for heights. Don't attempt in bad or windy weather, or after heavy rain (danger of rockfall or — very rarely — flash flooding). It can be very cold on this walk: be prepared! ***Don't lean on any handrails:*** *they are often loose, with rotted wood.* Signposting; some yellow/white waymarking

Equipment: walking boots, sunhat, sunglasses, suncream, raingear, long-sleeved shirt, long trousers, warm cardigan, warm jacket, gloves, swimwear, picnic, water

How to get there and return: 🚗 car or taxi to/from the parking area in the floor of the Barranco de las Angustias (see Car tour 3, page 26), then jeep taxi to Los Brecitos (they wait here for walkers; shared cost is about 10€ per person). *Note* that the taxis are only available from 08.30-12.30

Important notes: Permission is needed from the Parques Nacionales if you intend to stay in the national park overnight (obtain this at the visitor centre on the LP3 or tel: 922-497277), and you may camp *only* at the designated site. *Please don't follow the watercourses in this crater, as suggested in some books: they are too dangerous! Tourists have died as a result of following these watercourses.*

Shorter walk: Los Brecitos — Playa de Taburiente — Los Brecitos (9.5km/5.9mi; 3h10min). Moderate, with a descent/ascent of 400m/1300ft, otherwise grade as main walk. Equipment, access/return as main walk. Follow the main walk to the 1h20min-point and return the same way.

Alternative walk: Barranco de las Angustias — Cascada Colorada — Barranco de las Angustias (10.25km/6.4mi; 5h). Moderate, with an ascent/descent of some 550m/1800ft; much clambering over rocks and some paddling. Equipment as main walk. Access as main walk, but no jeep taxi necessary. From the parking area in the floor of the Barranco de las Angustias simply climb the bed of the *barranco*. Remain in this *barranco*, ignoring side-*barrancos* off to the left. This is the main walk in reverse; use the map to locate various landmarks. Beyond Dos Aguas, in the Barranco Río Almendro Amargo, be sure to turn right up the Barranco de Ribanseras rather than keeping left to the Playa de Taburiente. You will reach the waterfall shown on page 90 in 3h.

The Caldera de Taburiente *is* La Palma. If you don't spend at least a day in it, you haven't really seen the island. Streams tumble down from every *barranco*; indeed, these streams formed the *caldera* (crater), which at first was thought to be volcanic. Some ten kilometres (six miles) across at its widest point, and 2000 metres (over a mile) deep, Taburiente is one of the largest craters in the world to be formed by erosion. Recent studies, however, shy away from the crater theory, claiming it to be a massive landslide instead. It's one of La Palma's three natural wonders (the other two being the Ruta de los Volcanes and Los Tilos).

The walk starts at the car park in **Los Brecitos**: descend the path by a large NATIONAL PARK SIGNBOARD, pass through a turnstile, and head down into the *caldera*. Follow the path signposted 'ZONA DE ACAMPADA', ignoring all turn-offs. Hillsides tumble away below, and the rocky crater walls tower overhead, with pines clinging to the sheer slopes. *(Note that the pine needles are slippery underfoot.)* You cross a number of small *barrancos*, some with streams. The prominent peak rising out of the *caldera* wall

Looking up the Barranco de Ribanseras del Castro from just below its confluence with the Río Almendro Amargo (Cruce de Barrancos)

opposite is Pico Bejenado. Walk 10 goes to its very top.

A large boulder marks your crossing of the **Barranco de las Traves** (**35min**). More boulders begin appearing on the hillsides. The next ravine, the **Barranco de las Piedras Redondas** ('ravine of round rocks'), is well-named. The **Mirador del Lomo de Tagasaste**, from where you have a good view into the centre of the crater, follows. The deeply-gouged ravine of the **Barranco de Bombas de Agua** (**1h10min**) will either impress you or terrify you, or both, as you ascend the narrow path!

You finally arrive at the floor of the **Río Taburiente** at a wide basin known as the **Playa de Taburiente** (**1h20min**). Here you're enveloped by grand scenery. Small clumps of cool, shady Canary willow (*Salix canariensis*) stretch along the wide stony *playa*, where you can paddle in small pools. But the real prize of this hike is discovered 10 to 15 minutes downstream, where beautiful pools are hidden amidst huge boulders. The stream surges through them, crashing down in cascades. It's one of my favourite spots, and you are likely to have it all to yourself. The only drawback is that there is no proper path, and it is a difficult scramble to get there: keep to the left bank of the stream (facing downstream).

From the pools return to a point about 20m/yds short of where you originally entered the *barranco* bed on your descent from Los Brecitos (**1h50min**), and look out for a gap in the willows on your right (large SIGN-POST, plus yellow/white waymarking), to locate the path that ascends the western bank of the river to the CAMPING SITE above (**1h55min**). There

is an attractive stone-built services centre here (information, Red Cross first aid, guide services and toilets).

Keep to the left of the buildings (SIGNPOST); follow a path over to the edge of a cliff with a hair-raising view straight down to the Río Taburiente. The path continues over a col and soon Roque Idafe comes into sight, a prominent finger of rock balancing on the end of a ridge.

The **Somada del Palo** (**2h05min**), a signposted viewpoint on a nose of hillside jutting out into the plunging **Barranco del Río Almendro Amargo** ('bitter almond'), provides a fine perch over the river and equally good views back up to the heights of the crater. After about 25

Facing page: path beyond the camping area above the Río Taburiente, not long before reaching the Somada del Palo (top); the orange-yellow rocks at the Cascada Colorada in the Barranco de Ribanseras del Castro owe their colour to the iron content in the river (bottom). Above: in the Barranco de las Angustias, near Morro de la Era

minutes' descent on the steep, winding path, look back up the *barranco* for a good view of an aqueduct spanning the ravine. At the fork that follows five minutes later, keep right. A few minutes later the path that branched off to the left rejoins your route at **Las Lajitas del Viento**, from where you continue downhill.

Another signpost ('BARRANCO ALMENDRO AMARGO,

ROQUE IDAFE'; **2h45min**), marks the confluence of two streams. Head left here, scrambling down on all fours to the BED OF THE **Río Almendro Amargo**. Notice the rust-coloured water, caused by the high iron content. Follow this *barranco* to the left for a minute then, when it forks, continue to the right (noting the pretty waterfall) and ascend to the bed of the **Barranco de Ribanseras del Castro**. (*Note:* this stream needs to be crossed several times on loose slippery rocks, and the last two minutes are awkward and need care.) In 10 minutes you arrive at the 'coloured waterfall' shown on page 90 (**Cascada Colorada**; **3h**), a brilliant sight.

Return the same way from the cascade, but remain in the bed of the *barranco,* keeping downstream below the path from Cruce de Barrancos. Soon you arrive at **Dos Aguas** (**3h20min**), the confluence of the Almendro Amargo and Taburiente gorges. There is a giant grate on the left here, to collect debris from the river where it flows into a *canal.* Cross the Río Taburiente, then pick up the continuing path (at the right of a low concrete wall built across the **Barranco de las Angustias**; signpost: 'BARRANCO DE LAS ANGUSTIAS, SALIDA'). Continue downstream along this *barranco.*

Depending on the amount of water the river carries, you may have to leave the stream bed several times (some paths are signposted, others only marked with cairns). The first detour is just after a large pipe crosses the *barranco* above your head (at about **3h45min**). The second is signposted. The third is marked with cairns and a signpost 15 metres above the river bed. The fourth is on the *right-hand* wall. (Of course it is usually possible to stay in the bed of the *barranco,* getting your feet wet!)

Eventually you arrive at **Morro de la Era**, a derelict stone building. After returning to the *barranco* for five minutes, there's another detour up the left wall, then you descend once more to the *barranco* bed (**4h25min**). Before crossing the stream again from here, head *upstream* for two minutes, to a delightful pool and cascade hidden in a rocky corridor under a natural rock arch — most hikers miss this spot. After a final detour up the right wall, continue in the stream bed, which eventually dries up. Then you arrive at the main track; your car will be in the PARKING AREA a couple of minutes along to the left (**5h**).

12 FROM THE MIRADOR EL TIME TO PUERTO DE TAZACORTE

Distance/time: 3km/2mi; 1h05min

Grade: easy but steep descent of 600m/2000ft; not suitable in wet weather. You should have a head for heights, but the path is generally quite wide. *Red and white GR waymarking*

Equipment: walking boots, sunhat, sunglasses, warm cardigan, water, bathing suit (if you don't mind murky-brown seawater)

How to get there: 🚌 bus from Los Llanos (Línea 2) to the Mirador El Time; journey time 25min.

To return: 🚌 from Puerto de Tazacorte to Los Llanos (Línea 21); journey time 15min. Or return to Los Llanos on foot: follow the valley road for a little over 1km, to where signposting alerts you to the GR130 off right. Cross a footbridge and follow the red/white waymarked mule trail back to Los Llanos.

This walk is one long, continuous panorama. The vista stretches out over the Los Llanos plain and along the west coast to the south of the island. It's a short walk ideally done in the late afternoon, a great 'appetiser' for beginners.

Set out from the **Mirador El Time**, but first take in the superb panorama at this viewpoint. Small volcanic cinder cones stand out on the inclines, speckled with white houses, and banana plantations stretch for as far as the eye can see. The cliffs below you plunge down into the Barranco de las Angustias before it cleaves its way into the Caldera de Taburiente (Walk 11).

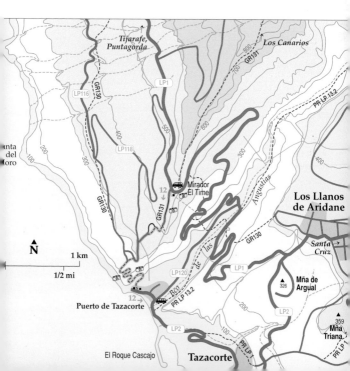

Walk downhill on the narrow road on the northwest side of the restaurant and souvenir shop (LARGE INFORMATION BOARD FOR THE GR131). The hillside below you is stepped in banana groves all the way to the sea-cliffs. When you reach the EDGE OF THE CLIFFS (**5min**) an even more expansive view unfolds, all the way up the Barranco de las Angustias and into the Caldera de Taburiente.

From the old cobbled camino real you have a superb view over Puerto de Tazacorte, spectacularly located at the mouth of the Barranco de las Angustias. Los Llanos is the village in the background to the left.

After a little over five minutes later, our way (which by now has reverted to track) leads through walled-in banana groves. Leaving the groves, ignore a path to the left; instead go right briefly, to round the hillside, following the good GR waymarking. A minute along, turn left downhill, to join a road and descend amidst greenhouses.

Descend to a T-junction and turn left (**20min**; signpost: 'GR131 PUERTO TAZACORTE'). Follow the road to the left, past park-sized gardens ablaze with colour and some ritzy homes enjoying a stupendous view. Three minutes down the road, turn left down a concrete ramp (SIGNPOST). After a minute on this path, flanked by high walls, the path joins the road again, before continuing downhill to the left (SIGNPOST).

From here you are walking into a picture-postcard. You edge along the rim of the plummeting Barranco de las Angustias, peering down onto Puerto de Tazacorte. From up here you can appreciate its beautiful location at the mouth of the *barranco*. On reaching the sea-cliffs, the way twists and winds down the sheer face of the escarpment. Don't walk *too* near the edge, as the cliffs drop away without warning … you might do the same! The descent is made even more impressive because of the beautifully-made path underfoot — an old cobbled *camino real*, which descends in zigzags. The sea along the harbour front is a murky brown, and the only colour in the little port below comes from the banana groves and attractive modern housing.

About half way down the cliffs (**40min**), the route veers left across the wall of the *barranco,* finally approaching the port from behind banana groves (beware of broken glass here). You enter **Puerto de Tazacorte (1h05min)** between a kiosk and a restaurant (one of the very few old buildings here). Walk along the promenade for 100m, then turn left into Calle Explanada and round the sunken plaza. Then bear right to the CASA DEL MAR bus stop.

13 TIJARAFE • PORIS DE CANDELARIA • TIJARAFE

Distance: 5.5km/3.5mi; 3h05min

Grade: very strenuous, with a descent/reascent of 650m/2100ft. You must be sure-footed and have a head for heights. Don't attempt in wet or windy weather. Although people *do* swim at Poris de Candelaria, I would not generally recommend it because of the swell. *Yellow and white PR waymarking throughout*

Equipment: walking boots, sunhat, sunglasses, suncream, warm cardigan, raingear, swimwear (just in case the sea is mirror-calm), picnic, plenty of water

How to get there and return: 🚌 from Los Llanos to/from Tijarafe (Línea 2); journey time about 45min. Or 🚗: park in Tijarafe and make your way to the Spar supermarket on the main LP1.

Alternative return to Tijarafe: After visiting Poris de Candelaria, go back to the 1h10min-point and take the narrow concrete road back up to Tijarafe. The time is approximately the same, but the ascent is easier.

Poris de Candelaria is an exquisite little hideaway. Supposedly, it was once used for just that purpose by pirates. Although there is a motorable lane down to this little cove, most drivers would find it far too hair-raising. If you're really fit, a far better way to get there is on foot, following this brilliant, if strenuous walk.

Start out in **Tijarafe**. From the BUS STOP, cross the street, walk uphill to the SPAR SUPERMARKET and take the first left immediately beyond it. Passing between the GUARDIA CIVIL and the CENTRO DE SALUD, the street narrows into a concrete lane and descends steeply, flanked by terraced plots. (*Beware* around here of dogs; I encountered a couple of nasty little ones lying in wait.)

At an INTERSECTION (**10min**), turn right on a track. Three minutes along, where the track bends right, turn left on a minor path. The path leads down alongside a rocky crest, with a *barranco* falling away on the left. Lone pines dot the grassy inclines. Small CAIRNS waymark the route

Right: coastal view about 30 minutes downhill. Below: descending to the 'pirates' cove (left); heading into the cove itself, where weekend retreats are built into the massive rock overhang.

now, all the way down to the sea.

On coming abreast of a GREENHOUSE on the opposite crest to the left (**25min**), the way forks. Go left (the paths rejoin, but the path to the left is much easier to follow). The path bends sharp left very briefly, then it keeps straight down the crest. The trail disappears from time to time, so *needs attention:* keep your eye out for the cairns. After about five minutes along the top of the ridge, the path descends the right-hand side of the crest, but without crossing the shallow *barranco* on the right. As you head over bedrock, move from cairn to cairn. A mixture of vegetation grows out of the grass: *tabaiba, taginaste, vinagrera, verode* and prickly pear.

You come to a point above a DRY CASCADE (**40min** or more, depending on your navigational skills), looking down over the rugged coastline. From here a neat cobbled path reveals itself zigzagging down the steep slopes below. Go left and descend a little, finally crossing the *barranco* below the cascade. The path is wide, but may still be unnerving for inexperienced hikers. Loose stones and gravel make this steep descent slippery, so take your time.

Ten minutes below the cascade, the path passes very close to the top of a cliff from where there is an excellent view across the plunging sea-cliffs to the northwest coast. Large clumps of the cactus-like candelabra spurge begin appearing on the seaward slopes. A number of small caves lie beside the path; nearer the shore many have been converted into sheds.

A path coming from the narrow concrete road joins your path (**1h10min**), and from here the good wide path shown on page 96 takes you down into the hidden cove, **Poris de Candelaria** (**1h15min**). Rounding the point, the most unexpected sight appears: an enormous shallow sea cave towers overhead. Weekend retreats, dwarfed by the 50m/150ft-high overhang, huddle around its base, just at the very edge of this tiny inlet. One almost expects Lilliputians suddenly to come out of hiding!

The bad news is: the homeward leg is 1h50min of sweat and tears. The good news is: when you reach **Tijarafe** (**3h05min**), beer will never have tasted better!

14 FROM TIJARAFE TO TINIZARA

See map opposite   **Distance/time:** 6km/3.5mi; 2h15min
Grade: easy-moderate, with ascents of about 300m/1000ft overall. *Red and white GR waymarking for most of the way*
Equipment: walking boots, sunhat, sunglasses, suncream, warm cardigan, raingear, picnic, plenty of water
How to get there: 🚌 from Los Llanos (Línea 2); alight one stop beyond Tijarafe village; journey time about 45min
To return: 🚌 same bus from Tinizara; journey time about 55min

My hiking companions call this the 'friendly hike', and so it is. Following bits and pieces of the *camino real* along the cultivated western shelf of La Palma, you seem to pass through everyone's back garden. The proud old cobbled trails weave their way amidst terraced plots of almond trees and dip into ravines in between them.

In the bus push the button, or shout 'Para aquí por favor', just after you pass the fishing boat 'in dry dock' on the right-hand side of the road outside the village of **Tijarafe**. **The walk begins** just northwest of the BUS STOP, some 50m/yds uphill from SUPERMERCADO CANDELARIA. Turn left down a road and then take the first right, heading through fields of almond trees with strips of vineyards and clumps of prickly pear in their midst. After two minutes, when the road swings left, turn right on a track (signpost: PUNTA GORDA, GR130, CAMINO REAL DE LA COSTA). Then turn left on a cobbled trail, rejoining the road two minutes later (SIGNPOST). Now follow the road downhill. Palm trees begin appearing, dotting the landscape. The terrain is very rocky, with many ravines concealed in the inclines. After two minutes, when the road curves left to descend the *barranco*, turn right (SIGNPOST) to climb the ravine on the old *camino*.

Soon (**10min**), flanked by an extravaganza of flowers, opposite a house, you meet a road. Cross straight over onto a path flanked by a high stone wall. Round the hillside on a clear path through almond groves, ignoring side paths. Seven minutes beyond the house, ignore a fork to the right, and immediately cross the **Barranco de la Cueva Grande**. Climb a splendid piece of old trail, and then emerge on a road, at a bend. Turn left downhill (SIGNPOST).

Ignore two entrances to private properties on the right and, at a junction two minutes down the road (where there is a WATER TANK on the left), keep straight ahead on a track (**25min**; SIGNPOST). Concrete comes underfoot briefly on this steep ascent. Pass a SHRINE on your right and, 50m/yds further on, come to a house. Take the track to the right of this house. Now the descent begins into the wild and picturesque **Barranco del Pinillo**, where there is a gigantic rocky protrusion in the ravine wall. Not far downhill, turn left on a path (SIGNPOST) and follow it down to the floor of the *barranco*. Creepers drape the ravine walls. On your ascent up the other side, Canary lavender lines the path. Abandoned, shuttered houses lie along the route.

Cross another (tiny) stream bed and soon pass a beautifully restored house (**45min**). Just after it, you come to two houses just above a road: climb the steps between them *(marked with a GR 'X' for 'wrong way', but perfectly viable)* and head straight up the hillside on a path. Ignore

Opposite: ascending to Tinizara on the camino real, *the old stone-laid trail. Above: attractive house with shrine*

the wider track on the left; keep following the cobbled path with the water pipes alongside it. Soon you pass by a rustic homestead undergoing restoration. On reaching the road again, in front of a large Canary palm, follow it downhill to the left, but don't forget to look back ocassionally, over the green hillsides descending to the sea, speckled with dark soldier-straight pines. In the distance lies the chain of volcanoes that punctures the island's southern spine.

Rounding a bend, about five minutes down the road, you'll see another palm tree on the right. Take the lower track that forks off right just below it, soon coming to a house. Go between the house and the garage, then continue from here on the barely-visible path behind the house, descending to the left over bare rock. You reach a road in a few minutes. Turn right on the road, into the ravine, where you come upon a lone pine on the left. Branch off left by this tree (SIGNPOST) on a trail that cuts down into the stream bed. You are on the *camino real* once more. At the fork a minute downhill, turn right uphill. A minute up, you come onto a concrete lane, just as it becomes tarmac (SIGNPOST). Follow this downhill.

Rounding the hillside, you cross another small ravine. At the SIGNPOST, turn right on a cobbled path. Small stone dwellings sit partially hidden in the rocky terrain, camouflaged by clumps of prickly pear cactus. Note the white powder on the prickly pear. It's the cochineal parasite, which used to be collected for its scarlet dye. After a couple of minutes along the path, turn right uphill to a road (**1h15min**; SIGNPOST) and pass the charming early

The ascent from the Barranco de la Baranda to Tinizara is the most picturesque stretch of the walk.

19th-century house shown above (on your right). Notice the shrine in the wall. After about five minutes the GR130 turns off to the right. (If you miss this turning, continue up the road for a little over 10 minutes, until it swings sharp right at the edge of a big ravine, the **Barranco de la Baranda**. A minute further up (SIGNPOST), you meet the GR130 and the *camino real* again. Follow it to the left uphill.) Soon the trail drops you down into a chasm — the deepest of them all, and a fine shady place to picnic. Cross a stream bed overgrown with blackberry bushes.

From here, the way to Tinizara is a steep climb, but the most picturesque section of the walk, up the fine old trail shown on page 100 (ignore all side-paths; continue straight up). Almonds wood the terraced hillsides. Just below the ROAD (**2h05min**), you pass a couple of traditional houses. Cross the road (SIGNPOST) and continue on the path. A minute up, reach the road again. Follow it to the left. After two minutes, turn up a wide path to the LP1 (SIGNPOST). The BUS STOP in **Tinizara** (**2h15min**) lies 50m/yds to the left. The local bar is a minute further along.

15 EL FAYAL • LAS TRICIAS • CUEVAS DE BURACAS • LAS TRICIAS

See also photograph page 2

Distance: 6.25km/4mi; 2h35min (2h05min for motorists)

Grade: relatively easy, with a descent of 400m/1300ft and ascent of 300m/1000ft. You must be sure-footed and have a head for heights. Not recommended in wet weather. *Red and white GR waymarking*

Equipment: walking boots, sunhat, sunglasses, suncream, warm cardigan, picnic, plenty of water

How to get there: 🚌 from Los Llanos to the turn-off for the El Fayal *zona recreativa* just beyond Puntagorda (Línea 2); journey time about 1h15min. Or 🚗: park in Las Tricias and use the map to join the walk at the 45min-point, less than 15min away, saving 30 minutes.

To return: 🚌 from Las Tricias to Los Llanos (Línea 2); same journey time

Las Tricias is known for two groups of residents — arboreal (the unique assembly of dragon trees) and human (the transient 'alternative life-stylers'). Both have become noteworthy curiosites in themselves, attracting tourists in droves. To avoid the crush, finish this walk before midday, and you'll be able to share the sights with just a few other people.

Begin the walk from the BUS STOP AT THE TURN-OFF FOR EL FAYAL: continue north along the road towards Las Tricias. The surrounding slopes are wooded in Canary pines. Three minutes along, you'll see a small white SHRINE below you, on the edge of the Barranco de Izcagua. Take the path down to the shrine and continue down into the *barranco* below (signposting: LAS TRICIAS). The path sidles down the sheer escarpment, where some guard rails lend psychological support *(but don't lean on them!)*. A stand of pine trees fills the valley floor. Ignore the path to the left. Ten minutes down, the way swings left and enters the bed of the **Barranco de Izcagua**. Not far down the stream bed, the path leaves it again, to ascend the right-hand bank.

Mount the crest, greeted by a grove of almond trees. Continuing along the edge of the *barranco*, ignore two turnings to the right (**25min**). A minute later, on joining a track, turn left (signpost: EL FAYAL, PUNTAGORDA, GR130, CAMINO REAL DE LA COSTA). Some 20m/yds downhill, turn right on a concrete track (signpost: LAS BURACAS, ST DOMINGO). When this track ends, the old path becomes your way again. Small country dwellings line the left side of this *camino*. Crossing a small *barranco*, you gain a first sighting of some large dragon trees on the hillside above.

This scattered little quarter of **Las Tricias** retains much of its original character. As you pass between some old homes with traditional high windows, chickens and cats scatter in all directions.

Emerging from the houses, you descend to the LAS TRICIAS ROAD, below the village centre. Cross a smaller road going left here and make your way down the main road to the right. A little over five minutes down the road (**45min**), just before it curves to the right, take the first cobbled lane on the left (signpost: LAS BURACAS, ST DO-MINGO). It passes between two houses, and you come onto

Dragon trees at Las Tricias, not far beyond the windmill shown on page 2

a track. Two minutes down the track, you pass through an intersection, and asphalt comes under foot. Just past the first house on the right, take the path descending to the right (signpost: 'RT TRAVIESA'). A minute down, opposite a house named LA CASA BLANCA, rejoin the road and follow it downhill for just over 100m/yds. At this point, where the road bends right, turn left on a path running along the edge of Barranco de Izcagua. Keeping straight down, pass rustic cottages set amidst colourful gardens and fruit trees. Although the hillsides are cultivated, they have a dishevelled appearance. More dragon trees appear.

Reach the road and turn left, making for an old windmill standing on the hilltop ahead (photograph page 2), by following the road to the left, then ascending a chained-off track on the right. A good vista awaits you from the WINDMILL (**1h05min**): the ridges flatten out on their descent before finally dropping into the sea. The ridge to the north is the refuge for the island's biggest concentration of dragon trees. Humble cottages lean up against the rocky ridge.

From here on a maze of paths will lead you through cosy corners of countryside. Facing inland, with your back to the windmill, take the path down the left side of the ridge, heading into prickly pear cacti. A minute down, on meeting a path, turn left. Passing below an ugly house that stands out like a sore thumb, you arrive at a junction of paths. Before continuing, admire the enormous dragon tree to the left. Then carry straight on through someone's garden and the outdoor 'living rooms' of some inhabited caves, to follow your path to the left; it descends the crest of the ridge.

Your next stop is the Buracas Caves, soon to be seen in the far wall of the *barranco* to the right. A good ten minutes down the ridge (having ignored several minor turn-offs left and right), you pass some low cottage rooftops on your left. Straightaway after this, take a clear path descending to the right. Just before another self-made house, follow the path to the right, round the wall of the *barranco*. In a few minutes you're standing in front of the **Cuevas de Buracas** (**1h30min**). The main cave is really just an overhang of rock. It's not much to look at, but a short way up the path beyond it there are a few more (equally unspectacular) caves, and some rocks marked with petroglyphs.

Home is all uphill! Return to the ridge and ascend it,

keeping to the crest. After 25 minutes you reach a track (SIGNPOST). Cross it (and the adjacent *canal*) and continue uphill on a cobbled path. You recross the track again a minute later (SIGNPOST). Heading up through almond trees, pass under a massive dragon tree. Joining another track, turn left to the road and follow this back up to LA CASA BLANCA, now on your right. Ascend the path opposite, and return along your outward route. Once back on the LAS TRICIAS ROAD (**2h15min**), follow it uphill for five minutes, until you see a concrete lane ascending between two houses on your left. Climb the lane and rejoin the road. Some 100m/yds up the road, turn left on a lane ascending the hillside. Then turn off the lane and follow a track up to the left, probably with a couple of crabby little dogs at your heels. You rejoin the road just below the village shop/bar in **Las Tricias** (**2h35min**); follow the road up to the left, to the BUS STOP in front of the village shop.

16 GARAFIA • EL PALMAR • JUAN ADALID
• EL PALMAR • GARAFIA

Distance: 13km/8mi; 4h05min

Grade: moderate, with ascents/descents of 400m/1300ft overall. Some short stretches demand a head for heights. Not recommended in wet weather. Can be extremely windy. *Red and white GR waymarking*

Equipment: walking boots, sunhat, sunglasses, suncream, warm jacket, raingear, picnic, plenty of water

How to get there and return: 🚌 from Los Llanos to/from Garafía (Línea 2); journey time 1h45min. The return bus leaves Garafía from alongside the petrol pumps near the plaza. Or 🚗: park in Garafía near the *plaza*.

Short walk: Garafía — El Palmar — Garafía (6.25km/3.9mi; 1h40min). Easy, with ascents/descents of 200m/650ft overall. Otherwise grade, equipment and access as main walk. Follow the main walk to El Palmar and return the same way.

The north of the island remains relatively untouched by tourism. Being far from the main tourist centres, it hasn't become a hiking highway like the Ruta de los Volcanes or the Caldera de Taburiente. It's wild and rugged, with villages few and far between.

You leave the bus in **Garafía** at the turning for the village centre. From the BUS STOP walk straight to the *plaza* (main square). The church is worth a visit if you have the time (see touring notes on page 18). Then locate the *farmacía* behind the church, where **the walk begins**. (There is a large, confusing sign here in three languages; read the part for the GR130.) Follow the small road uphill past the pharmacy for 50m/yds, then turn left on a cobbled path descending into the **Barranco de la Luz** (signpost: EL PALMAR, BARLOVENTO, GR130, CAMINO REAL DE LA COSTA). First you'll notice the dragon trees. Large clumps of the cacti-like candalabra spurge grow out of the *barranco* walls too.

The path crosses the bed of the *barranco* and climbs out the far side (this ascent may be unnerving for those who have no head for heights). You pass two houses built into the hillside, and emerge on the end of a CONCRETE TRACK (**10min**). Keep ahead on the track for two minutes, then turn right on a path. Two minutes later, back on the track (SIGNPOST), turn right but, after under 30m/yds, pick up the old *camino* again, below the track. You pass through two wooden gates; please close them behind you. You round the hillside, passing through traces of terracing. Open and spacious, devoid of settlement and with windswept vegetation, this is La Palma's 'wild (north)west'. Soon the rocky shoreline comes into view.

Passing above an uninhabited homestead, descend to

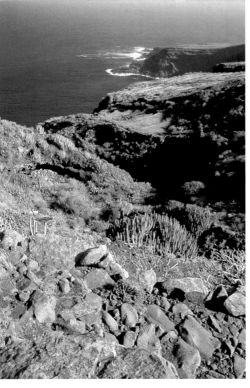

At about 35 minutes into the walk, approaching El Palmar, you look across the northwest corner of the island (left) and may spot a lonely billy goat (right). A corral lies just below the path at this point (far right).

a track and follow it to the right for 20m/yds. Then pick up the path again, on the left. Solitary houses dot the sides of ridges. The terrain is rocky; little grows here except for the usual xerophytic vegetation. Ignore a turning left (**35min**) and ascend to a track (SIGNPOST). Follow this downhill to the left. Two minutes down, turn right to rejoin the old path. Two minutes further along, when you are overlooking a homestead, the way forks. Both paths descend to the track just below, the left fork being easier. The *barranco* here is full of candalabra spurge.

On the bend just before the homestead, ascend the path to the right (signpost: EL MUDO, BARLOVENTO), walking alongside a pink *casita*. A few renovated and derelict cottages lie below. This is **El Palmar**, and soon you arrive at the edge of the deep **Barranco El Palmar** (**50min**). *(The Short walk returns from here.)*

Pass through the intersection at the edge of the *barranco* and descend into the ravine. Bare posteriors may appear out of the caves down in the *barranco:* these are just 'alternative life-stylers' — nothing personal, they're not mooning. Approaching the floor of the *barranco,* keep left. Then walk along the stream bed to the right, to a *fuente* (spring) hidden behind enormous yam leaves. The water is refreshingly cool but, unfortunately, the spring is dry in summer.

From the *fuente* return along the *barranco* bed for 10m/yds, where your path out of the *barranco* ascends to the right. Climbing the wall of this ravine, you pass a deep cave. Ignore the turning to the right just past the cave. A stiff climb takes you up to a COUPLE OF HOUSES (**1h10min**). Pass above them and, two minutes later, walk behind another house. Don't forget to enjoy the view behind you: a pleasant feeling of isolation spreads over these hills. A minute later you join a minor, unused track. Two minutes uphill, when this track bends right, turn left onto the old *camino* again. The few houses you can see strung out along the edge of the *barranco* opposite comprise the hamlet of El Mudo. A couple of minutes along, the path joins a minor track: keep ahead (SIGNPOST). The tops of wind generators now appear over the crests of the ridges ahead. Some five minutes later, you come to the MAIN TRACK (**1h25min**) that descends to El Mudo (signpost: JUAN ADALID, BARLOVENTO). Follow this track to the right uphill for a minute, then rejoin your path by scrambling a couple of metres up the bank on the left (SIGNPOST). The surrounding hillsides are covered in cistus and heather.

One final, deep ravine follows — the **Barranco Domingo Diaz**. A blade of ridge jutting into the sea below, surmounted by a chapel, catches your attention on this fairly vertiginous, but amply wide path. Amazingly enough there's a track up to the chapel. At the bottom of the *barranco*, please close the GATE (**1h55min**) after you, as you are entering an enclosure. Climbing out of the *barranco,* the way is blocked by fences and another gate. Go through the gate and follow the path through a 'tunnel' of heather. Beyond the heather, you look across a shallow gully onto a couple of farm houses dwarfed by seven giant wind generators. Quite a sight! Cross a farm track, and dip into the gully, ignoring the turning to the left.

Passing to the right of a house, the path arrives at a road in **Juan Adalid** (signpost: DON PEDRO, BARLOVENTO). Turn left downhill, then turn left again on the track to the WIND GENERATORS and climb the HILLOCK beyond them (**2h 10min**). If there isn't a gale blowing, this is the perfect spot for a picnic. A couple of lonely outposts lie on a coastal shelf below. Looking across the northern coastline, severed by sheer cliffs, the village to the east is Gallegos (Walk 1).

From here retrace your outward route back to **Garafía** (**4h05min**).

17 PISTA AL DERRABADO • SABINOSA • ERMITA DE LA VIRGEN DE LOS REYES • SABINOSA

Distance/time: 15km/9.5mi; 5h40min

Grade: very strenuous, with an ascent of about 700m/2300ft and descents of 1300m/4250ft overall. You must be sure-footed and have a head for heights. Don't attempt in wet weather. It can be very windy and cold on this walk, and the *cumbre* is often covered in cloud.

Equipment: walking boots, sunhat, sunglasses, suncream, long-sleeved shirt, long trousers, jacket, raingear, picnic, plenty of water

How to get there: 🚌 from Tigaday/Frontera towards Valverde (Timetables EH1 and EH2); alight at the Pista al Derrabado; journey time 20min. Or taxi or with friends to the Pista al Derrabado.
To return: 🚗 Telephone to Tigaday for a taxi from the bar in Sabinosa.

Short walks

1 Pista al Derrabado — Sabinosa (6.5km/4mi; 2h05min). Quite easy, with a descent of 600m/2000ft. Short stretches demand a head for heights, otherwise grade as main walk. Access and equipment as main walk, but stout shoes will suffice. Follow the main walk to Sabinosa, the 2h05min-point. Telephone for a Tigaday taxi from Bar Sabinosa.

2 Sabinosa — Ermita de la Virgen de los Reyes — Sabinosa (8.5km/5mi; 3h35min). Very strenuous, with an ascent of 650m/2100ft. Grade and equipment as main walk. Access by 🚗: park in Sabinosa. Join the walk at the 2h05min-point and follow it to the end.

This far-flung corner of the island is for me the most beautiful part of El Hierro. Once over the cloud-enshrouded *cumbre*, and no longer battered by wind, you can traipse across a little corner of the island's 'Cornwall', where sheep and cows are the only company you'll have. If you're not made of marathon material, the two short walks are both well worth considering.

Start the walk at the junction with a track, the **Pista al Derrabado** (signposted 'FUENTE DE MENCAFETE'). From here you have a splendid view across the banana and pineapple plantations of El Golfo to the rocky islets of

Ermita de la Virgen de los Reyes

Salmor. **Set off** by following this track: it gradually descends around the sheer face of the escarpment, into the **El Golfo** crater. The hills are thickly wooded in laurel. The western part of the crater is bare of life save for the veins of stone walls that cross it. A spa, the Pozo de la Salud, is marked by a large, prominent building standing above the sea. At one point (**35min**) you have an uninterrupted view through a gap in the vegetation over the western wing of the crater. Pass through farmland set on shelves high in the wall of the *cumbre*. A good 20 minutes later, at a fork, go left (signposted 'FUENTE MENCAFETE').

Attention: Around five minutes uphill, an ENCLOSED PROPERTY sits off the track to the right (**1h**). Just beyond it, be sure to leave the track, following a grassy overgrown path downhill (signposted 'SABINOSA'). You round a steep hillside, passing above a farm shed. You will remain on this path all the way to Sabinosa: ignore a number of minor paths turning off. You come to a stone BENCH (**1h20min**) — a good rest stop. Just past it, as you round a bend, a bird's-eye view unfolds down onto the picturesque but rather severe looking Sabinosa, atop a volcanic mound that protrudes from the crater wall. The dark volcanic slopes that surround it are patched in vineyards. The descent of these gravel slopes may prove slightly unnerving for some.

When you reach a street in **Sabinosa** (**2h**) keep straight ahead to Camino la Dehesa. Then go right downhill on Calle Hoya del Moral (the lower half of Camino la Dehesa). At the *plaza* turn right to the friendly local, Bar Sabinosa (**2h05min**), to revive yourself for the tough ascent ahead. *(Short walk 1 ends here, and Short walk 2 begins here.)*

Return to Camino la Dehesa and now climb it. It circles above the village. Just where it begins to descend, turn left uphill on a well-maintained path signposted 'Camino a la Dehesa' (yellow/white waymarking). Then, at a fork, keep left. A steep climb through vineyards and then heather follows, with no turn-offs to worry about. Dark green junipers dot the lower inclines. Don't forget to enjoy the views behind you. On reaching the tree-heather and evergreen zone, you may be enveloped in cloud — notice the rocks and tree trunks beside the path, thick with moss. Nearing the *cumbre* the way is again slightly vertiginous. This is where you feel the full brunt of the wind, too.

Just over the CREST (**3h 20min**), by a spring on the left, you meet the end of a track. You overlook a pastoral landscape here, littered with old lichen-clad stone walls. Below to the right, clumps of pine trees make a half-hearted attempt to forest an uneven basin. If you have any energy left, make for these pines — out of the wind and, with luck, in the sun — as idyllic a spot as you'll find on the island.

To continue to the Ermita de la Virgen de los Reyes, keep straight along the track, ignoring tracks to the left and then the right. Some 15 minutes along, take a rough track descending to the right (the **Camino de la Virgen**; signposted).

You reach the **Piedra del Regidor** at a junction of tracks. (Every four years, the July 'Bajada de la Virgin' begins here at dawn.) A right turn here leads to the Mirador de Basco and El Sabinar. Take the second track to the left (white/red waymarking). The track cuts through an old crater. Five minutes along, just after the road becomes surfaced, turn left down a paved walkway to the **Ermita de la Virgen de los Reyes (3h55min)**, home of the island's patron saint.

From here retrace your steps back to **Sabinosa**, allowing about 1h45min for the return (**5h40min**).

Top: in the heather and evergreen zone, on the ascent to the Ermita de la Virgen de los Reyes. Bottom: view down over Sabinosa on the descent from the Pista al Derrabado

18 FRONTERA • MIRADOR DE JINAMA • ERMITA VIRGEN DE LA PEÑA • LAS PUNTAS

See also photograph page 10

Distance/time: 12km/7.5mi; 5h05min

Grade: strenuous, with an ascent of 900m/3000ft and a steep descent of 700m/2300ft. You must be sure-footed and have a head for heights. The walk is only worth the effort on clear fine days. Take care when crossing any loose gravel, whether it is on the path itself or the result of a landslide. Don't attempt after heavy rain; there is a danger of rockfall. It can be very windy on the top of the *cumbre*.

Equipment: walking boots, sunhat (tied on!), sunglasses, suncream, long-sleeved shirt, long trousers, walking stick(s), warm cardigan, anorak, raingear, picnic, plenty of water

How to get there: 🚗 by taxi or with friends to Frontera (or walk there from the Tigaday/Las Puntas junction.
To return: 🚗 Telephone for a Tigaday taxi, from the phone box or nearby bars at Las Puntas.

Short walks

1 Mirador de Jinama — Frontera (4km/2.5mi; 1h35min). Easy, but steep descent of 900m/3000ft. Otherwise grade and equipment as main walk. Access by 🚌 from Tigaday/Frontera towards Valverde (Timetables EH1 and EH2); alight at the Mirador de Jinama turn-off; journey time 35min. Follow the road to the *mirador*, 10min away, then descend the signposted path to Frontera. Use the map to do the main walk in reverse. From Frontera, either call a taxi from Tigaday or walk back.

2 Mirador de la Peña — Las Puntas (4km/2.5mi; 2h15min). Fairly easy, with an initial steep ascent of 150m/500ft, followed by a descent of 700m/2300ft. Otherwise grade and equipment as main walk. Access by 🚌 from Valverde towards Guarazoca (Timetable EH3); alight at the Mirador de la Peña; journey time 20min. Return as main walk. Refer to the map to climb to the Las Puntas turn-off above the Ermita Virgen de la Peña (25min), then follow the main walk from the 3h35min-point.

Alternative walks

1 Frontera — Mirador de Jinama — San Andrés (8km/5mi; 2h50min). Ascent, equipment, access as main walk. Return by 🚌 from San Andrés (Timetables EH1 and EH2) or telephone a Tigaday taxi from there. Follow the main walk to the country road beyond the Mirador de Jinama. Seven minutes along this road, turn right on a wide path signposted 'PR EH8, San Andrés' (white-yellow waymarking). Some 30min from the road, and shortly after the path has widened to a track, turn right at a fork. Almost immediately, turn left on another track. A minute later, when a track joins you from the right, follow it to the left (signposted 'GR131, Tiñor–Valverde, Camino de la Virgen'). Just around the bend, turn right onto the old path again. Several minutes later, cross the Guarazoca road and enter San Andrés, passing the school and the church. The bus stop is outside the shop on the left, where you meet the main HI1.

2 Frontera — Mirador de Jinama — Mirador de la Peña — Las Puntas (12km/7.5; 5h). Grade, equipment and access as main walk, *but this walk is slightly more difficult* (although the vertiginous stretches can be avoided by crossing fields). A spectacular cliff-top route. Follow the main walk to the country road beyond the Mirador de Jinama but, almost immediately, fork left on a wide dirt track. In 15min it ends: now just follow the cliffs for just under an hour and a half. Keep *well clear* of the cliff-edge, which could crumble away. Scramble over any walls with the *utmost care,* so as not to dislodge any stones, and look carefully before crossing any fields: bulls don't like intruders! Meeting the track above the Ermita Virgen de la Peña, turn left past the site of an old quarry. Some 45m/yds below the quarry, turn left to descend to Las Puntas: pick up the main walk at the 3h35min-point.

This hike is one long view. From beginning to end you overlook the most stunning bay of the archipelago, El Golfo. And if that's not enough, the magnificent path underfoot is one of the most breathtaking in all the Canaries ... both literally and visually.

The bus drops you in the tiny village of **Frontera**. To

begin the walk, take the small road between the two bars opposite the church. At the fork 10m/yds uphill, keep left, following the sign 'JINAMA 3.4KM'. A steep concrete lane takes you up a hillside stepped with vineyards. An amphitheatre of precipitous walls encircling the entire bay rises up before you. Your path will climb this very wall! A couple of minutes after passing a parking area with a couple of benches, the concrete lane bends sharp right (**10min**). At the bend, turn left up a wide cobbled path (signposted). This fine centuries-old trail will take you up to the *mirador*. At a fork keep left and, on reaching the lane again, go left for 20m/yds, then rejoin your path. Thick stone walls flank the *camino*. Cross the lane one last time, by a sign, 'CAMINO DE JINA-MAR' (**20min**).

Above the vineyards the route dives into shady laurel woods. The higher the climb, the more striking the views. The distant splash of white, high up the mountain wall near the end of the *cumbre,* is Sabinosa. The path, a work of art, ascends in a string of tortuous Zs. Here the preciptous cliffs are home to some rare endemics: *Bencomia sphaerocarpa, Crambe strigosa* and *Sideritis canariensis,* as well as the more common *Echium strictum* and *Aeonium holochrysum.*

A BALCONY VIEWPOINT (**1h20min**) makes a good rest stop, looking across the coastal plain of *malpais*. Pineapples are cultivated in the numerous greenhouses spread across it. The surrounding vegetation drips with moss and lichen. After ignoring a minor fork to the left, as you near the summit, a couple of unstable-looking stone tables and benches at a hillside *mirador* (**1h50min**) provide a superb view over the gulf, framed by the *cumbre*. Fifteen minutes later, you reach the **Mirador de Jinama** (**2h05min**; Picnic 18a), with a fountain (sometimes dry) in the hillside on the right, to the right of a chapel, the **Ermita de la Caridad**. *(Short Walk 1 begins here.)* From the *mirador* you enjoy a superb view out over the whole bay, a dark lava coastline with jagged indentations contrasting with the bright greens and blues of the sea. The *cumbre* sweeps back out of the bay into a high wall fringed in laurels and heather.

From here the way is all downhill. Follow the road away from the *mirador*. When it swings right towards the main road, continue straight on along a country road. *(Alternative walk 2 now turns left almost immediately; Alternative Walk 1 turns right off this road after seven minutes.)* Now you're on the roof of the island, looking across a sloping plateau ruptured by a multitude of small volcanic cones. A maze of stone walls criss-cross the landscape. Thirty minutes down the road, just after passing a fenced-off garden opposite a pint-sized VOLCANO (a good viewpoint; **2h35min**), turn left along a wide track. The track bumps its way between walled-off fields and grazing land, with the occasional plot of corn or potatoes.

Some five minutes along, just before the track comes to a dead end, turn right on another track flanked by stone walls. On meeting the ROAD again (**3h05min**), follow it to the left downhill for 200m/yds, then pick up your continuing path, which passes behind a MASSIVE WATER

TANK. A minute along you come to the end of a track. Follow this track for 50m/yds, to where it turns right; here keep straight ahead on a minor track, which soon bends left. Again go straight ahead, to pick up the old *camino* (between high stone walls). At the fork ahead, keep right on the main path. A few houses of Guarazoca can now be seen on the hillsides far below.

Less than 20 minutes from the road, you drop down onto a colourful, pink and mauve earthen track. Turn left along it, and a good 10 minutes later, as you are passing below an old quarry (**3h35min**), turn right down an asphalt lane at the edge of the crater. After 45m/yds, you

*View down onto
the Roques de
Salmor from the
rim of the crater
(near Picnic 18b)*

reach the turning left to Las Puntas (signpost: 'PR EH8,
Camino de la Peña'). *(Short Walk 2 joins the route at this
point.)* The path disappears over the cliff face. Your first
thought is ...wow! Before setting off, continue down the
lane for another minute to the **Ermita Virgen de la Peña**,
tucked into the side of the cliff just below. This chapel is
a superb quiet spot from which to enjoy the immense
panorama (Picnic 18b; photograph page 10).

If you wish, now visit the Mirador de la Peña, which
you can see from here: follow the concrete lane down to
the road, 15 minutes away, and turn left. (Add 40 minutes
to the walking times, if you take this detour.)

Return to the Las Puntas turn-off above the chapel.
(Alternative Walk 2 rejoins the main walk here.) Wind
steeply down the cliff-hanging path, looking across to the
the Roques de Salmor. Las Puntas is straight below you,
and the lone village seen near the far western end of the
crater is Sabinosa (Walk 17). Some people will find this
descent vertiginous, although the path is amply wide. But
the path *is* prone to rockfall, and somewhere along the
descent you will have to scramble gingerly over scree. At
the time of writing there were several landslides to be
crossed, all of which were passable. *Do* use your
common sense: if the path looks in the slightest bit
dangerous, due to more recent landslides, abandon the
descent — a taxi from the top will be a lot cheaper than
the local hearse from the bottom.

About five minutes above the road, the path forks: the
left fork is easier. Reaching the road at **Las Puntas** (**5h
05min**), you'll find a bar five minutes along to the right,
and a telephone kiosk a few minutes further along, on the
left side of the road.

19 HI1 • MIRADOR DEL LA LLANIA • HOYA DE FILEBA • FUENTE DEL LOMO • BAILADERO DE LAS BRUJAS • HI1

Distance: 5km/3mi; 1h10min

Grade: easy, with an ascent of less than 100m/330ft; suitable for all fit people

Equipment: walking shoes, warm cardigan, jacket, long trousers, raingear, water

How to get there and return: 🚐 from Tigaday/Frontera towards Valverde (Timetables EH1 and EH2); alight/reboard at the turn-off to the Ermita de la Virgen de los Reyes; journey time 30min. Or by 🚗: park alongside the HI1 at the same place.

This short hike is El Hierro's little gem. It starts with yet another stupendous view over the gulf — a view of which I never tire. Then it wanders in and out of 'fairy-tale' woods, where you feel you've stepped centuries back in time. Moss envelops the trees and thickly carpets the ground. And the crater of Hoya de Fileba comes as a pleasant surprise.

Alight from the bus on the HI1 at the JUNCTION FOR THE ERMITA DE LA VIRGEN DE LOS REYES. **Start out** by crossing the road and following the path signposted 'MIRADOR DE LA LLANIA' into the tall tree-heather. A short climb leads up to the **Mirador de la Llanía** (5min; Picnic 19), a superb vantage point looking down over the line of villages strung out along the foot of the *cumbre*. The forested walls of the crater stretch out impressively on either side.

From this bald piece of gravelly hillside, follow the sign for 'BAILADERO DE LAS BRUJAS' (the Witches' Dancing Ground). The path edges its way through a small wood, the vegetation dripping with lichen and moss. Out on the *lapilli*-covered slopes again, ignore a path ascending to the left. Barely a minute further down this steep slope, the path swings left to dip down into a small hollow of pine trees. Here, at a signposted junction, keep straight ahead, taking a zig and a zag up a steep slope, to the edge of a deepish crater — the **Hoya de Fileba** (15min). This charcoal-grey crater is speckled with heather.

Top: overlooking the Hoya de Fileba, reached after 15 minutes. Right: view down into El Golfo from the Mirador de la Llanía (Picnic 19)

Return to the signpost and now turn left for 'FUENTE DEL LOMO'. Look a short way along the road to the right, for a culvert. Walk through the culvert, then ascend the embankment on the left and continue along the path. Join a wider path and follow it to the right, to be greeted in a few minutes by a water tank — the **Fuente del Lomo**. Unlike any other spring I've come across, you step *down* into this one.

With your back to the tank, take the path to the right, following a sign for 'EL FAYAL' (orange arrow). Almost immediately, at a junction, turn right. The slopes above the path are cushion-soft with moss, tempting you run your hands over the inclines. At a faint crossing, with signpost and arrows, go left. Mounting a slight rise, an old track with stones placed intermittently on either side comes underfoot. When you come to a cool grassy clearing with a signpost, cross a wide path and continue straight ahead on the right-hand side of the clearing along a path lined with stones. Follow this path, ignoring all side-paths and tracks; your path is intermittently marked with orange arrows.

You cross two small but noticeable gullies, the second on a WOODEN BRIDGE (**45min**). The vegetation changes and patches of laurel forest take over from the heather. Not far beyond the bridge, you cross the HOYA DEL MORCILLO ROAD and continue on the path signposted 'LA LLANIA'. At the fork that follows, wind your way up to the right. Ignore a path to the left as you follow the stone path-liners and a small gully running alongside on the right.

One minute before reaching the ROAD TO THE ERMITA DE LA VIRGEN DE LOS REYES (**1h**), at a cairn and a signpost with an arrow, take a path to the right. (But before doing this you may like to go onto the road and follow it to the left for a striking view of the volcanic landscape.)

Returning to the cairn, keep on along the path, parallel with the road, ignoring all turn-offs. After a couple of minutes, you're dwarfed by a towering lone pine and swallowed up amidst laurel wood and heather. A few minutes later, at a crossing, go right and then almost immediately left; this path leads takes you back to the HI1 (**1h10min**), just where the walk began.

20 HI1 • MIRADOR DE LAS PLAYAS • LA TORRE • SAN ANDRES • ARBOL SANTO • TIÑOR

Distance/time: 18km/11mi; 4h50min

Grade: easy but very long, with short ascents of about 200m/650ft overall. Suitable for anyone who is fairly fit. *Note:* these highlands can often disappear under cloud and mists, and it can be cold and windy; the walk is best kept for fine, cloudless days.

Equipment: walking boots, sunhat, suncream, raingear, long-sleeved shirt, long trousers, warm cardigan, anorak, swimwear, picnic, plenty of water

How to get there: 🚐 from Tigaday/Frontera towards Valverde (Timetables EH1 and EH2); alight at the turn-off for the Ermita de la Virgen de los Reyes; journey time 30min
To return: 🚕 prearrange for a taxi to collect you from the junction of the HI1 and the road into Tiñor, on the north side of the village.

Short walk: San Andrés — Arbol Santo — San Andrés (8km/5mi; 1h50min). Easy; equipment as above, but walking shoes will suffice. The above weather conditions apply. 🚐 from Tigaday/Frontera to/from San Andrés (Timetables EH1 and EH2); journey time 40min. (Or return by taxi.) By 🚕: park in San Andrés. Follow the main walk from San Andrés (the 3h-point) to the Arbol Santo, then return the same way.

Shorter walk: HI1 — Mirador de las Playas — La Torre — San Andrés (11km/6.75mi; 3h). Easy; equipment and access as main walk; return as the *Short walk*. Follow the main walk to San Andrés.

Alternative walk: HI1 — Mirador de Isora — Parador (13km/8mi; 4h25min). Strenuous, with a steep, rough descent of 800m/2600ft from the *mirador* (tough on the knees). You must be sure-footed and have a head for heights. Do not attempt in wet or very windy weather. Yellow/white waymarking. Equipment and access as main walk; to return, telephone for a taxi from the *parador*.
Follow the main walk to Tajace de Abajo (1h55min). As you come upon the houses, turn right immediately after building No 3 (opposite house No 4). There is a signpost here, 'PR EH3, Las Playas, La Cuesta, Vereda del Risco'. Follow an asphalted road straight downhill until you reach the road to the *mirador*, below Isora. Follow this road to the right for 10min, to the Mirador de Isora (2h25min). Your ongoing path (flanked by stone walls) begins on the far side of the viewpoint (signposted), and ascends to the crest opposite — then you begin the descent. A couple of minutes from the *mirador*, ignore a faint turning to the right. *Take utmost care* as you descend this very steep and slippery path, and leave any gates as you find them. Some 1h35min from the *mirador*, just before entering the bed of the Barranco del Abra, a

This orange track, edged with asphodels, leads through bucolic countryside to the Arbol Santo.

path joins you from the right; keep left downhill. The next 20 minutes are spent floundering in and out of the stream bed, until you reach the road. The *parador* is less than 15min along to the right.

The pine trees in El Pinar are among the most majestic in the archipelago. Just as bonsai is striking in its contrived, pint-sized beauty, so the *Pinus canariensis* is striking in its natural grandeur. From the heights of El Pinar you descend to another of El Hierro's picture-postcard *miradors*, before gradually climbing to a countryside where time stands still. If you're the adventurous type, I highly recommend the Alternative walk.

Start the walk at the TURN-OFF TO THE ERMITA (Santuario) DE LA VIRGEN DE LOS REYES. Just at the start of this road, take the path to the left signposted 'SENDERO DE LA MEDIANIA' and follow it to where it crosses the HOYA DEL MORCILLO ROAD. Join the road and turn right. By an ENORMOUS PINE (**25min**), note a track turning left into the forest. Pass it by but, 90m/yds below it, at a bend in the road, turn left on a minor track. After 50m/yds, at a fork, go left. You dip into a hollow to the left, then mount a second, parallel crest. After 50m/yds, ignore a track to the right. This track will take you straight down to the El Pinar road. (Even if you lose trace of the track, just keep straight down to reach the road.) In this cool, shady forest, grand pines surround you. The forest floor is 'whistle-clean', a characteristic of a true Canary wood. A little over five minutes down the track, cross a *canal*. Less than 10 minutes later you cross the EL PINAR ROAD (HI4): keep straight on towards the stone wall ahead, crossing a water pipe en route. Then turn left alongside the wall and, without a path, remain between the pipe and the wall (closer to the pipe in the last few metres) until, after 15 minutes, you meet the ROAD TO THE MIRADOR DE LAS PLAYAS. Turn right here, passing the turn-off right for Las Casas almost immediately. After a few minutes you reach the **Mirador de las Playas** (**1h05min**; Picnic 20). It overlooks the desolate isolated corner of the island shown below. The narrow curving bay set at the foot of 1000m/ 3300ft-high eroded cliffs is Las Playas. The *parador* is an obvious landmark in this harsh corner.

From the *mirador* return along the road for 200m/yds, then take a path (signpost: 'PR EL3 LAS PLAYAS, LA CUESTA') which initially dips down, before heading uphill between stone walls. The small evergreen shrub predominant in the fields here is white broom *(escabon)*. Less than 20 minutes from the *mirador* you join a track very near the edge of the cliff. This becomes asphalted and soon ascends to a ROAD (**1h35min**; signpost: 'PR EL3 LAS PLAYAS, LA CUESTA'). Turn right on the road and, a minute along, turn right again to climb nearby **Montaña Bermeja**,

Picnic 20 and Alternative walk 20: plunging view from the Mirador de las Playas down onto the isolated Playas, a curving line of stony beaches hidden in the sheer coastline. The parador *and a few solitary houses are the sole occupants of this barren, inhospitable stretch of arcing coastline.*

Crossing the plateau through walled-in pastures, on the approach to San Andrés

an orange volcanic mound. From its summit there are fine views over the farming village of Isora on the slopes ahead.

You will now continue along this quiet country road for around 30 minutes, to La Torre. *(But if you are doing the Alternative walk, turn off the road about 20 minutes downhill, opposite house No 4 in Tajace de Abajo.)*. In **La Torre** (**2h05min**) you cross a concrete ford in the road. Barely two minutes later, turn left along a road called CALLE LA LADERA, passing a beautifully-restored cottage after 100m/yds. When you join a road ascending from the right, continue uphill. Some 15 minutes from La Torre (**2h20min**), take the first left, a track which ascends a narrow *barranco*. A minute up, an old cobbled *camino* becomes your way. The path climbs alongside the gully, before entering it briefly. Ignore minor side-paths. Two minutes up the gully, leave it (beside a volcanic cone), and continue towards the left as the path crosses a plateau. Ignore a turn-off left (**2h40min**). The path widens into a track. When you meet the road, turn right onto the wide path. Walled-in pastures stretch across this tableland. San Andrés comes into sight across the stone walls, spread around the base of a volcanic cone.

Soon you cross a wide dry stream bed (also a junction): keep right here. Then, a little further on, keep left along a wide track. Remain on this track until you reach a road on the edge of **San Andrés**. Follow the road to the left and, after a few minutes, you come to the MAIN ROAD (**3h**). I enjoy the noisy back-slapping BAR LA IGUALDAD along to the right. *(The Short walk starts here, and both the Short walk and the Shorter walk end here.)*

Leaving San Andrés (from Bar La Igualdad), cross the road and follow it to the west (left), then take the first street (Calle La Iglesia) to the right. Follow it to the Las Montañetas road and turn right. After 150m/yds, turn right on a wide track (signpost), soon passing a row of volcanic cones on the right. You come to a junction: keep right (signpost: 'GR131, PR EH7, Tiñor, Valverde, El Garoe, El Mocanal, La Caleosa'). A little over five minutes later (**3h20min**), fork left uphill on asphalt (sign: Arbol Santo). *(Note that you will return to this junction after your visit.)* The way is tarred only for the first few minutes, then the beautiful earthen track shown on pages 124-125 becomes your way. A basin of stone walls lies below to the right, and on the left volcanic mounds grow out of a tilting plateau. After 20 minutes, at the next fork, go left downhill (signposted 'Arbol Santo/Garoe'). A tarred road leads you down to a parking area/visitor centre, from where a well-trodden path heads right, round the hillside to **El Garoé**, the site of the original 'holy tree' (**Arbol Santo**; **3h50min**). Legend has it that the original tree, a *til* (indigenous laurel), was venerated by the native Bimbaches as their 'rain tree', because it condensed enough water from the mists to fill all their requirements. Remains of the cisterns that collected the water can still be seen in the hillside. *(The Short Walk returns to San Andrés from here.)*

Now on the leg to Tiñor, return to the fork first encountered at the 3h20min-point (less than 30 minutes

Top: near La Torre; bottom: El Pinar (left) and one of the old cisterns near the Arbol Santo.

back; **4h20min**; signpost: 'GR131, Tiñor, Valverde'. Turn sharp left here, across a sheltered basin. After a good five minutes, ignore a faint track to the left. Minutes later, at a staggered junction, first turn left off the main track and then, at the fork that follows, keep right along a cobbled trail. Above lie fields of *tagasaste* (broom); its branches are cut for animal fodder. Soon you cross the main road (HI1) and descend to **Tiñor**, a quiet hamlet tucked away in a concealed valley. Entering the village, pass the church and cross a road, to continue on the path, which descends to a driveway. Follow the drive back to the road, then keep straight on (right) for a couple of minutes, to regain the HI1 main road (**4h50min**). Here you can flag down the bus, or pick up your taxi.

BUS TIMETABLES, FLIGHTS AND FERRIES

LA PALMA — BUSES

For a list of all 16 of the island's bus lines, with timetables and a good route map, see **www.transporteslapalma.com**. If you will be using the buses frequently, invest in a 'Bonobus' card (12 €); this will save about 20% on bus fares; several people can use the same card.

Line 1: Santa Cruz — Los Llanos (via the *cumbre*)

Bus passes the visitors' centre 40min from Santa Cruz, 20min from Los Llanos.

Departs Santa Cruz	Departs Los Llanos
06.15**	06.30**
07.15	07.30
08.15**	08.30**
08.45*	09.00*
09.15	09.30
10.15**	10.00*
10.45*	10.30**
11.15	11.00*
11.45+	11.30
12.15**	12.00*
13.15	12.30**
14.15*	13.30
15.15	14.30*
16.15*	15.30
17.15	16.30*
18.15*	17.30
19.15	18.30*
20.15*	19.30
21.15*	20.30*

Line 1A: Los Llanos — El Paso

Departs Los Llanos	Departs El Paso
06.30**	07.00*
07.30	08.00
08.30**	09.00**
09.00*	09.30*
09.30	10.00
10.00*	10.30*
10.30**	11.00**
11.00*	11.30*
11.30	12.00
12.00*	12.30*
12.30**	13.00**
13.00*	13.30*
13.30	14.00
14.00*	14.30*
14.30*	15.00*
15.30	16.00
16.30*	17.00*
17.30	18.00
18.30*	19.00*
19.30	20.00
20.30*	21.00*
21.30	22.00*

Line 2: Santa Cruz — Los Llanos (via the north, usually with a change of bus in Barlovento) — *Intermediate times are approximate!*

Santa Cruz	La Galga	Los Sauces	Barlo-vento	Gallegos	Punta-gorda	Taza-corte	Los Llanos
			06.00*	06.15*	07.30	07.45	08.15
06.15*	06.45*	07.00*	07.30*	07.45*	09.30*	10.15*	10.45*
07.15	07.45	08.00a					
08.15*	08.45*	09.00*	09.30*	09.45*	11.30*	¨12.15*	12.45*
10.15	10.45	11.00	11.30	11.45	13.30	14.15	14.45
12.15*	12.45*	13.00*	13.30*	13.45*	15.30*	16.15*	16.45*
14.15	14.45	15.00	15.30	15.45	17.30	18.15	18.45
16.15*	16.45*	17.00*	17.30*	17.45*	19.30*	20.15*	20.45*
18.15	18.45	19.00	19.30	19.45b			
20.15*	20.45*	23.00a					
22.30	22.45	23.00a					

Los Llanos	Taza-corte	Punta-gorda	Gallegos	Barlo-vento	Los Sauces	La Galga	Santa Cruz
			06.45*	07.30	07.50	08.20	08.50
			08.30*	09.30*	09.20*		09.50*
06.15*	06.30*	07.30*	08.45*	09.30*	09.50*	10.20*	10.50*
08.15	08.30	09.30	10.45	11.30	11.50	12.20	12.50
10.15*	10.30*	11.30*	14.45*	13.30*	13.50*	14.20*	14.50*
12.15	12.30	13.30	14.45	15.30	15.50	16.20	16.50
14.15*	14.30*	15.30*	16.45*	17.30*	17.50*	18.20*	18.50*
16.15	16.30	17.30	18.45	19.30	19.50	20.20	20.50
18.15*	18.30*	19.30*	20.45*b				
20.15	20.30	21.30c					

*Mon-Fri only; **not Sun or holidays; a terminates at Los Sauces; b terminates at Franceses, 15min from Gallegos; c terminates at Puntagorda

131

Line 3: Santa Cruz — Los Llanos (via Los Canarios, Fuencaliente, Mazo)

Buses depart Mazo approximately 20min from Santa Cruz, 55min from Los Llanos; Los Canarios 40min from Santa Cruz, 40min from Los Llanos; Fuencaliente 45min from Santa Cruz, 30min from Los LLanos

Departs Santa Cruz	Departs Los Llanos
06.00*	06.00*
08.00	08.00
10.00	10.00
12.00	12.00
13.15* (only to Mazo)	14.00
14.15	16.00*
16.00	18.00
18.00	20.00
20.15	
22.30	

Line 4: Los Llanos — Puerto Naos

Buses from Los Llanos go on to Charco Verde; buses from Puerto Naos depart from Charco Verde 10min earlier

Departs Los Llanos	Departs Puerto Naos
06.30**	07.00**
07.30**	08.00**
08.30	09.00
09.00**	09.30**
09.30	10.00
10.00**	10.30**
10.30	11.00
11.00**	11.30**
11.30	12.00
12.00**	12.30**
12.30	13.00
13.00**	13.30**
13.30	14.00
14.00**	14.30**
14.30	15.00
and every hour on the half hour daily until	and every hour on the hour daily until
22.30	23.00

Line 8: Santa Cruz — Airport

Departs Santa Cruz	Departs Airport
06.45*	07.15
07.15	07.45*
07.45	08.15
08.15*	08.45*
08.45	09.15
09.15*	09.45*
09.45	10.15
10.15*	10.45*
10.45	11.15
11.15*	11.45*
11.45	12.15
12.15*	12.45*
12.45	13.15
13.15*	13.45*
13.45	14.15
14.15*	14.45*
14.45	15.15
15.15*	15.45*
15.45	16.15
16.15*	16.45*
16.45	17.15
17.15*	17.45*
17.45	18.15
18.15*	18.45*
18.45	19.15
19.15*	19.45*

Line 21: Los Llanos — Puerto de Tazacorte (via Tazacorte)

Departs Los Llanos	Departs Puerto Tazacorte
06.30**	07.00**
07.30**	08.00**
08.30	09.00
and every hour on the half hour daily until	and every hour on the hour daily until
22.30	23.00

Línea 12 Los Sauces — San Andrés (via Espindola)

Los Sauces	San Andrés	San Andrés	Los Sauces
07.10*	07.25	07.30*	07.55
09.10	09.25	09.30	09.55
11.10	11.25	11.30	11.55
12.10*	12.25	12.30*	12.55
14.00	14.15	14.20	14.45
17.10	17.25	17.30	17.55

*Mon-Fri only; **not Sun or holidays

EL HIERRO — BUSES

Buses are run by the Sociedad Cooperativa de Transportes (14, Calle El Molino, Valverde). At time of writing they did not have a web site, but timetables could be downloaded at **www.ecoturismocanarias.com/hierro/es** (click on 'Transporte'; then, from the *Spanish* page, click on 'Horarios' — the English page may not load properly). The seven routes used in this book are below, but see overleaf for details of six new routes.

EH1 Sabinosa — Tigaday/Frontera — Valverde *Mon, Thu, Sat**

Sabinosa	Tigaday/Frontera	Valverde
06.30	07.50	08.40
Valverde	Frontera/Tigaday	Sabinosa
12.00	12.50	14.10

*only runs via the *cumbre* on Sat; Mon and Thu via Guarazoca

EH2 Las Puntas — Tigaday/Frontera — Valverde *Wed, Fri*

Las Puntas	Tigaday/Frontera	Valverde
06.30	07.35	08.25
Valverde	Frontera/Tigaday	Las Puntas
12.00	12.50	13.55

EH3 Guarazoca (Mirador de la Peña) — Valverde *Mon-Sat*

Guarazoca	Valverde
07.45	08.05
15.40a	16.00a
Valverde	Guarazoca
12.00	12.20
14.30a	14.50a

EH4 Isora — Valverde (via La Cuesta and Tiñor) *Mon-Sat*

Isora	Valverde
07.30	07.55
15.15a	16.10a
Valverde	Isora
12.00	12.25
14.30a	14.55a

EH5 La Restinga — El Pinar (Taibique) — Valverde *Mon-Sat*

La Restinga	El Pinar (Taibique)	Valverde
07.00	07.30	08.15
Valverde	El Pinar (Taibique)	La Restingua
12.00	12.40	13.20
14.30a	15.10a	15.50a

EH6 La Caleta — Valverde (via Tamaduste) *Sun only*

La Caleta	Valverde
19.00	19.30
Valverde	La Caleta
09.00	09.30

EH7 Valverde — Aeropuerto *Mon-Sat*

Valverde	Aeropuerto
09.15	09.30
Aeropuerto	Valverde
08.55	09.10

a not Sat

Six new bus routes have recently been introduced, using small buses (19 places).

Sabinosa: departs bus station *(estación de guaguas)* in Valverde 09.30 and 13.00 (Mon-Fri); departs Sabinosa 09.45, 13.15

Las Puntas: departs bus station *(estación de guaguas)* in Valverde 09.00 and 13.15 (Mon-Fri); departs Las Puntas 09.15 only

Frontera–Mocanal–Valverde–airport: Departs Frontera 07.30 (Mon-Fri); runs via the tunnel

Frontera–San Andrés–Norte–Valverde: Departs Frontera 07.00 (Mon-Sat); on Mon-Fri via Guarazoca, on Sat via the Cumbre

La Restinga–Pozo de la Salud: Departs La Restinga 08.00 (Mon-Fri); runs via El Pinar, Tigaday, Sabinosa

Pozo de la Salud–La Restinga: Departs Pozo de la Salud 13.00 (Mon-Fri); runs via Sabinosa, Tigaday, El Pinar

DIRECT FLIGHTS TO LA PALMA

At time of writing there are direct flights from London Gatwick and Manchester to Santa Cruz de la Palma on Mondays throughout the year. For infomation see www.thomsonfly.com.

INTER-ISLAND TRAVEL

You can travel between the islands by air or ferry but, unfortunately, arrangements seem to change every year — some years the only direct connection is by air, other years by ferry.

By plane: At time of writing it is *not* possible to fly direct between the islands — one has to travel via Tenerife or Gran Canaria. Flights are frequent and connections good, making a total journey time of about two hours. Still, that compares very badly with the direct flights which used to run twice a week and take only 15-20 minutes!

Keep your eye on the web site **www.bintercanarias.com**, to see if the direct flights have been resumed. All information about current flights via Tenerife or Gran Canaria is on the same web site, and flights can can be booked online — or contact your travel agent *before you go* (flights may be full if you wait until you are on the islands to book).

By ferry: At time of writing there is one direct ferry a week (Sundays at 17.00) from La Palma to El Hierro, and three direct ferries a week from El Hierro to La Palma (Tuesdays at 03.45, Thursdays at 05.30, Saturdays at 09.00). The crossing time is about 3h45min. For details of these direct sailings, see **www.navieraarmas.com**.

Otherwise it is fastest to travel via Tenerife. Two ferry companies currently serve these routes: Naviera Armas (as above) and Fred Olsen Lines (**www.fredolsen.es**).

A third company, Trasmediterranea (**www.trasmediterranea.es**), used to sail between La Palma, Tenerife and El Hierro — and may well start again, so it is always worth looking at their web site, too!

Ferry bookings can be made online, at travel agencies before you go or once you are on the islands — or at the ferry kiosks at the Santa Cruz and Valverde ports.

● Index

This index contains geographical entries only; for other entries, see Contents, page 3. **Bold type** indicates a photograph; *italic type* indicates a map. Both may be in addition to a text reference on the same page. 'TT' refers to *timetable numbers* (see pages 131-134).